Adobe®
Muse™
onDemand

Ted LoCascio

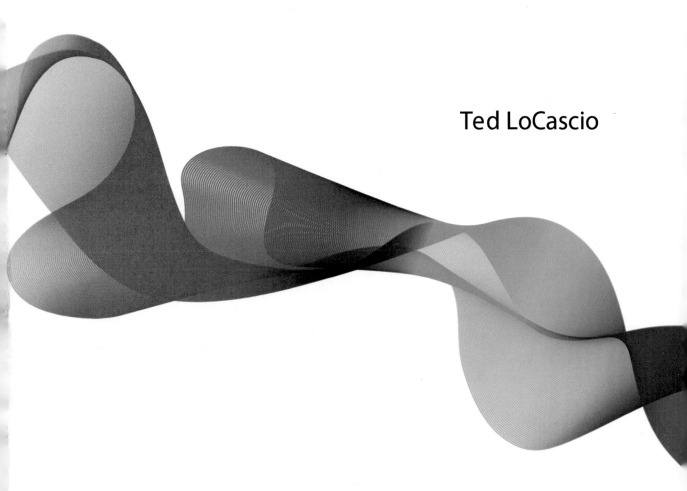

Que® Que Publishing, 800 East 96th Street, Indianapolis, IN 46240 USA

Copyright © 2012 by Pearson Education, Inc.

All rights reserved. No part of this book shall be reproduced, stored in a retrieval system, or transmitted by any means, electronic, mechanical, photocopying, recording, or otherwise, without written permission from the publisher.

No patent liability is assumed with respect to the use of the information contained herein. Although every precaution has been taken in the preparation of this book, the publisher and author assume no responsibility for errors or omissions. Nor is any liability assumed for damages resulting from the use of the information contained herein.

The Library of Congress cataloging-in-publication data is on file.

ISBN-13: 978-0-7897-4842-3
ISBN-10: 0-7897-4842-8

Printed and bound in the United States of America
First Printing: June 2012

Que Publishing offers excellent discounts on this book when ordered in quantity for bulk purchases or special sales.

For information, please contact:

U.S. Corporate and Government Sales
1-800-382-3419 or corpsales@pearsontechgroup.com

For sales outside the U.S., please contact:

International Sales
1-317-428-3341 or International@pearsontechgroup.com

Publisher
Paul Boger
Editor-in-Chief
Greg Wiegand
Acquisitions Editor
Laura Norman
Development Editor
Todd Brakke
Managing Editor
Kristy Hart
Project Editor
Jovana Shirley
Copy Editor
Gill Editorial Services
Indexer
Cheryl Lenser
Proofreader
Debbie Williams
Editorial Assistant
Cindy Teeters
Cover Designer
Anne Jones
Compositors
Ted LoCascio
Nonie Ratcliff
Technical Editor
Christine Ricks

Acknowledgments

Ted LoCascio

First and foremost, I must thank everyone at Que Publishing and Pearson Education for making this book possible. Thanks to associate publisher Greg Wiegand and to acquisitions editor Laura Norman for sharing my vision on this project and for being as genuinely enthusiastic about Adobe Muse as I am. Thanks also to Christine Ricks for acting as my technical editor and making sure every step, shortcut, and tip is correct.

Special thanks to my copy editor, Karen Gill at Gill Editorial Services, for making this book read as well as it does. I must also thank my project editor, Jovana Shirley, for working with me on the book's schedule and keeping everything on track.

Loving thanks to my wife, Jill, and to my sons, Enzo and Rocco, for being so patient while I was busy writing this book. Thanks also to Mom, Dad, Val, Bob and Evelyn Innocenti, and the rest of my extended family for being so supportive.

And of course, thanks to the Adobe Muse development team for making such great software to write about.

Dedication

To my wonderful wife, Jill, and our two sons Enzo and Rocco, for their never-ending love and support.

About the Author

Ted LoCascio is a professional graphic designer, author, and educator. He served as senior designer at the National Association of Photoshop Professionals (NAPP) for several years and has created layouts, graphics, and designs for many successful software training books, videos, websites, and magazines. Ted is the author of numerous graphics software training books and videos and has contributed articles to *Photoshop User* magazine, Creativepro.com, the Quark Xtra newsletter, PlanetQuark.com, indesignsecrets.com, and *InDesign Magazine*. He has also taught at the Adobe CS Conference, the InDesign Conference, the Pixel Conference, the Vector Conference, and PhotoshopWorld. A graphic designer for more than 15 years, Ted's designs and illustrations have been featured in several national newsstand and trade magazines, books, and various advertising and marketing materials. For more about Ted LoCascio, please visit tedlocascio.com.

We Want to Hear from You!

As the reader of this book, *you* are our most important critic and commentator. We value your opinion and want to know what we're doing right, what we could do better, what areas you'd like to see us publish in, and any other words of wisdom you're willing to pass our way.

We welcome your comments. You can email or write to let us know what you did or didn't like about this book—as well as what we can do to make our books better.

Please note that we cannot help you with technical problems related to the topic of this book.

When you write, please be sure to include this book's title and author as well as your name and email address. We will carefully review your comments and share them with the author and editors who worked on the book.

Email: feedback@quepublishing.com

Mail: Que Publishing
        ATTN: Reader Feedback
        800 East 96th Street
        Indianapolis, IN 46240 USA

For more information about this book or another Que title, visit our website at informit.com/register. Type the ISBN (excluding hyphens) or the title of a book in the Search field to find the page you're looking for.

Contents

Introduction

Welcome to *Adobe Muse on Demand*, a visual quick reference book that shows you how to work efficiently with Muse. This book provides complete coverage of basic to advanced Muse skills.

How This Book Works

You don't have to read this book in any particular order. We've designed the book so that you can jump in, get the information you need, and jump out. However, the book does follow a logical progression from simple tasks to more complex ones. Each task is presented on no more than two facing pages, which lets you focus on a single task without having to turn the page. To find the information that you need, just look up the task in the table of contents or index, and turn to the page listed. Read the task introduction, follow the step-by-step instructions in the left column along with screen illustrations in the right column, and you're done.

How You'll Learn

How This Book Works

Step-by-Step Instructions

Exercise Files

Get Updates

Adobe Software

Workshops

Step-by-Step Instructions

This book provides concise step-by-step instructions that show you how to accomplish a task. Each set of instructions includes illustrations that directly correspond to the easy-to-read steps. Also included in the text are time-savers, tables, and sidebars to help you work more efficiently or to teach you more in-depth information. A "Did You Know?" provides tips and techniques to help you work smarter, whereas a "See Also" leads you to other parts of the book containing related information about the task.

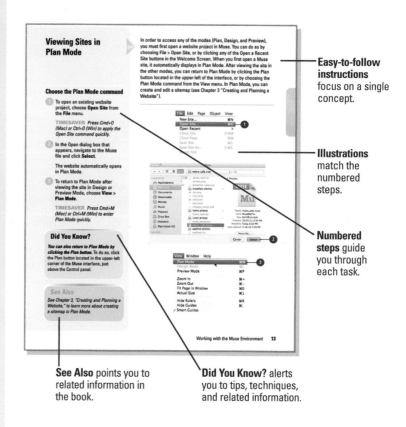

Easy-to-follow instructions focus on a single concept.

Illustrations match the numbered steps.

Numbered steps guide you through each task.

See Also points you to related information in the book.

Did You Know? alerts you to tips, techniques, and related information.

Exercise Files

The Workshops section of this book uses exercise files that are available to you. You can locate these files on the Web by navigating to www.queondemand.com. By following along with the exercise files, you won't waste time looking for or creating your own assets. Note that not every task requires an exercise file, and some require the use of your own images.

Exercise files enable you to follow along with the steps.

Get Updates

Like any software, Muse continues to change and get better with updates and patches, so it's important to regularly check the Adobe Muse site at muse.adobe.com.

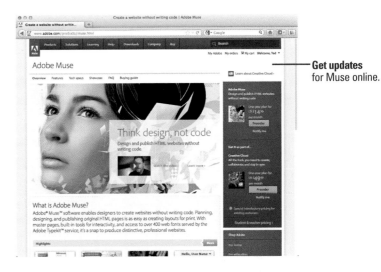

Get updates for Muse online.

Adobe Software

Muse is part of the Adobe software family, and can be used in conjunction with Photoshop CS6, Photoshop CS6 Extended, and Fireworks CS6. For more info about Photoshop, Fireworks, and the Adobe Creative Suite, please visit www.adobe.com/products/creativesuite.html.

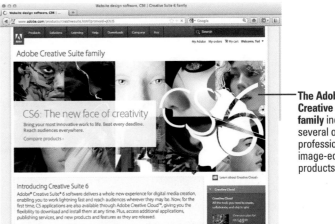

The Adobe Creative Suite family includes several other professional image-editing products.

Workshops

This book shows you how to put together the individual step-by-step tasks into in-depth projects with the Workshop. You start each project with a sample file and then work through the steps. The Workshop projects and associated files are available on the Web at www.queondemand.com.

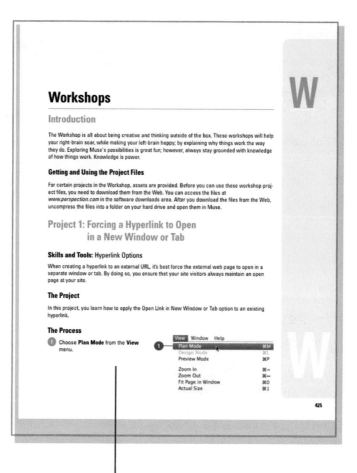

The **Workshop** walks you through in-depth projects to help you put Muse to work.

Getting Started with Adobe Muse

Introduction

Adobe Muse is designed specifically for us. You know who you are. You're the designers who learned to create dynamic layouts visually and have no desire to work with HTML code. Some of us are scared to death of code. Others have learned HTML out of necessity, but can't stand the thought of working with it. Many of us come from a print design background and are struggling to keep up with the modern age of web design and all it entails.

Whether we like it or not, the design world is evolving into a screen-based marketplace. The term "graphic designer" now assumes that you are well versed in Dreamweaver and HTML code. Yet there is nothing creative about tinkering with code, now is there? How did our creative jobs become so complicated and (gulp) mathematical? I hate math! Don't you?

Thankfully, the good folks at Adobe have not forgotten us. With Muse, Adobe has given us the freedom to create dynamic websites without ever even having to look at code. The Muse interface behaves very similarly to working with Adobe InDesign. Muse even includes familiar print design-oriented features such as master pages, site-wide styles, and round-trip editing with Photoshop.

With this first chapter, you'll learn how to acquire a yearly Muse subscription, as well as how to download, install, and launch Muse.

What You'll Do

Acquiring a Muse Subscription

Installing Muse

Launching Muse

Acquiring a Muse Subscription

Muse is only available for purchase via subscription. You can pay for Muse on a month-to-month basis or by purchasing a discounted yearly subscription. This subscription-based service enables the Adobe Muse development team to add new features to the software regularly, rather than asking you to wait a year or more to acquire them via a purchased upgrade.

Purchase a month-to-month or yearly subscription

1. Using your preferred web broswer, visit www.adobe.com/products/muse.

2. Click the **Buy** button.

3. In the shopping window, choose the preferred plan (**One-year** or **Month-to-Month**).

4. Click the **Add to Cart** button.

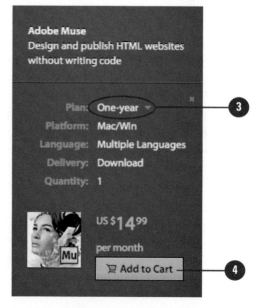

5 In the My Cart page that loads in your browser, click the **Checkout** button.

6 In the Subscription Terms and Conditions page that loads in your browser, you must agree to the terms and conditions and then click the **Checkout** button.

7 In the Checkout page that loads, enter your Sign in credentials (email and password), and click **Sign in**.

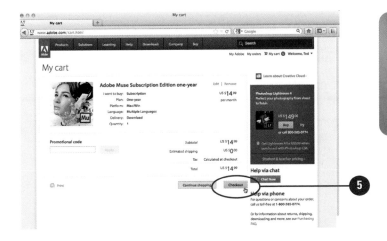

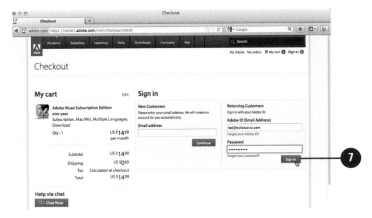

8 Enter the correct information in the **Billing and Payment** fields of the Checkout page.

9 Click the **Review Order** button.

10 After reviewing your order, click the **Place Order** button.

By clicking Place Order, you acknowledge that as a condition to install and use your Adobe product, you must agree to the terms of Adobe's click-through product license agreement (including any third party terms which may appear in the agreement).

Installing Muse

Install Muse with the Adobe Application Manager

1. After you purchase Muse from the Adobe online store, Adobe gives you access to the Muse installer. To download the installer, click the **Download** button.

2. To download the Muse Installer, you must create a free Creative Cloud account. To do so, click **Join the Creative Cloud**.

3. To gain access to all of the applications in the Creative Cloud, choose a monthly payment plan. To access Muse alone at no extra charge, click **Start for Free**.

After you purchase a Muse subscription from the Adobe online store, you can then download the Adobe Application Manager and install Muse. Muse is part of the Creative Cloud online service; therefore, you must create a free Creative Cloud account in order to download the Adobe Application Manager and install Muse. Note that you will always have access to the Adobe Application Manager installer at your account at Adobe.com. This can be helpful should you ever need to download the installer again and reinstall the software.

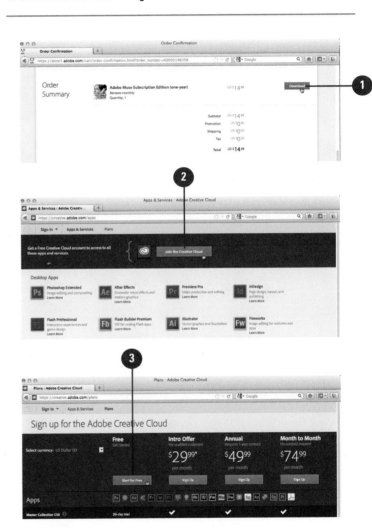

4 In the Join the Creative Cloud page that loads in your browser, enter your Adobe ID and password.

5 Click **Sign In**.

6 In the Terms of Use window that loads in your browser, you must agree to the terms and conditions and then click the **Accept** button.

7 In the Apps & Services column of the new page that loads, click the **Muse** button under Desktop Apps.

8 In the Desktop Apps page that loads, click the **Download** button.

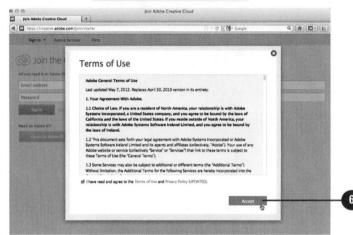

9. In the window that appears, click **OK** to download the Adobe Application Manager.

10. Click **Save File**.

11. Double-click the AdobeApplicationManager.dmg file.

12. Double-click the AdobeApplicationManager installer.

   The application installs automatically on your system.

13. Enter your Adobe ID and password.

14. Click **Sign In**.

15. In the Adobe User Agreement window that appears, click **Accept**.

16 In the Adobe Application Manager, click the **Adobe Muse Install** button.

The Adobe Application Manager downloads and installs Muse on your system.

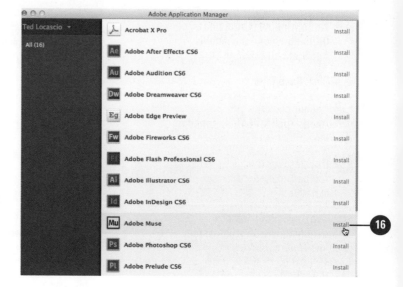

Launching Muse

If you've made it this far, then you must have successfully purchased, downloaded, and installed Muse on your system. The next step is to launch the application for the first time—then you can begin learning how to utilize this exciting new web design tool!

Launching Muse in Mac OS X

1 From the Finder, choose **Applications** from the **Go** menu.

> **TIMESAVER** *Press Shift+Cmd+A to apply the Go to Applications command quickly.*

2 In the Finder window that appears, double-click the **Muse** icon.

After you launch the application, the Muse interface appears with the Plan module and Welcome Screen displayed.

Did You Know?

You can also launch Muse from the Dock. To do so, you must first save the Mu icon in the Dock. First, launch the application as described above. Then click and hold the Muse icon in the Dock and choose Options > Keep in Dock. After it is saved, you can click the icon in the Dock to launch the application.

Muse launches and displays the Welcome Screen.

Launching Muse in Windows XP/Vista/7

1. Click the **Start** button on the Taskbar.

2. Click **Adobe Muse**.

After you launch the application, the Muse interface appears with the Plan module and Welcome Screen displayed.

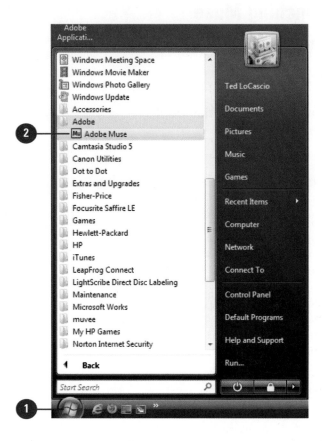

Muse launches and displays the Welcome Screen.

Working with the Muse Environment

Introduction

After purchasing, downloading, and installing Muse, the next step is to become familiar with the application's interface. There are various interface modes, panels, and tools you can use to plan and design your websites.

In this chapter, you'll learn how to locate and access Plan Mode, which is where you can create a sitemap to build your website's page structure and hierarchy. Plan Mode is also where you can access master pages. With master pages, you can ensure that any repeating page elements, such as nav bars and footers, maintain their position throughout your site.

This chapter also explains how to enter Design Mode, where you can create and edit your website's individual web pages and master pages. You'll learn where the Design Mode tools are located and how you can access them quickly with keyboard shortcuts, as well as how to expand and collapse the Design Mode panel column. In addition, you'll learn how to change the view percentage of the current page so that either its entire content area fits in the window, or the page is displayed at actual size as it would appear in a browser.

In the final sections of this chapter, you'll learn how to show and hide rulers, page guides, header and footer guides, smart guides, and the page grid overlay.

Working with the Welcome Screen

By default, the Welcome Screen appears automatically each time you launch Muse or close the current website you are working on. By clicking the Site button, you can create a new website project (see Chapter 3, "Creating and Planning a Website"). You can also reopen any existing websites you've recently worked on by clicking any of the buttons located under the Open a Recent Site column. To access the Muse website, click the Learn More About Muse button on the right side of the window; to access Muse updates, click the update button in the lower-right corner.

Show and hide the Welcome Screen

1. The Welcome Screen appears automatically each time you launch Muse or close all the websites you are currently working on.

2. To hide the Welcome Screen, click the close button in the upper left corner of the window.

Did You Know?

You can choose not to show the Welcome Screen when launching Muse or closing a site. To do so, you must enable the Don't Show Again option located in the lower-left corner of the Welcome Screen. After you enable this option, simply close the Welcome Screen as described in Step 2 above. From this point forward, the Welcome Screen does not appear when you launch Muse or close the current website.

Did You Know?

You can also hide the Welcome Screen using Preferences. To do so, choose Muse > Preferences (Mac) or Edit > Preferences (Win) and uncheck the Show Welcome Screen option.

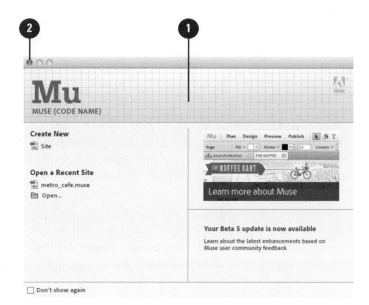

Viewing Sites in Plan Mode

In order to access any of the modes (Plan, Design, and Preview), you must first open a website project in Muse. You can do so by choosing File > Open Site, or by clicking any of the Open a Recent Site buttons in the Welcome Screen. When you first open a Muse site, it automatically displays in Plan Mode. After viewing the site in the other modes, you can return to Plan Mode by clicking the Plan button located in the upper-left of the interface, or by choosing the Plan Mode command from the View menu. In Plan Mode, you can create and edit a sitemap (see Chapter 3 "Creating and Planning a Website").

Choose the Plan Mode command

1. To open an existing website project, choose **Open Site** from the **File** menu.

   TIMESAVER *Press Cmd+O (Mac) or Ctrl+O (Win) to apply the Open Site command quickly.*

2. In the Open dialog box that appears, navigate to the Muse file and click **Select**.

   The website automatically opens in Plan Mode.

3. To return to Plan Mode after viewing the site in Design or Preview Mode, choose **View > Plan Mode.**

   TIMESAVER *Press Cmd+M (Mac) or Ctrl+M (Win) to enter Plan Mode quickly.*

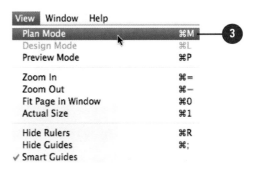

Did You Know?

You can also return to Plan Mode by clicking the Plan button. To do so, click the Plan button located in the upper-left corner of the Muse interface, just above the Control panel.

See Also

See Chapter 3, "Creating and Planning a Website," to learn more about creating a sitemap in Plan Mode.

Viewing Sites in Design Mode

In Design Mode, you can use the various tools and panels to create and edit your website's individual pages. You can enter Design Mode at any time by choosing the Design Mode command from the View menu or by clicking the Design button located in the upper-left corner of the interface. To open a specific web page or master page in Design Mode, you must double-click the page's thumbnail in the Plan Mode sitemap.

Choose the Design Mode command

① To open a website project in Design Mode, choose **Design Mode** from the **View** menu.

   TIMESAVER *Press Cmd+L (Mac) or Ctrl+L (Win) to apply the Design Mode command quickly.*

   If you do not already have additional pages or master pages open in Design Mode, Muse automatically displays the Home (index) page.

   IMPORTANT *To open a specific page or master page in Design Mode, you must double-click the page thumbnail from the Plan Mode sitemap.*

Did You Know?

You can also return to Design Mode by clicking the Design button. To do so, click the Design button located in the upper-left corner of the Muse interface, just above the Control panel.

Muse automatically displays the Home (index) page in Design Mode.

Open a specific web page in Design Mode

① To open a specific web page in Design Mode, you must return to the sitemap in Plan Mode by choosing **View** > **Plan Mode**.

TIMESAVER *Press Cmd+M (Mac) or Ctrl+M (Win) to apply the Plan Mode command quickly.*

② Double-click the page thumbnail from the Plan Mode sitemap.

Muse displays the selected page in Design Mode.

Did You Know?

You can also return to Plan Mode by clicking the sitemap tab in Design Mode. The sitemap tab displays the name of the website project on it, preceded by the sitemap icon. To return to the sitemap, click the sitemap tab located in the upper-left corner of the interface, just below the Control panel.

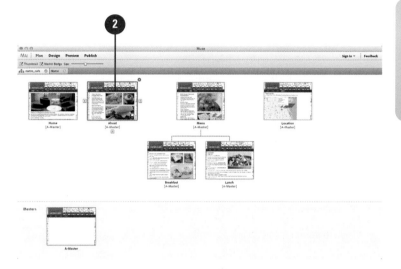

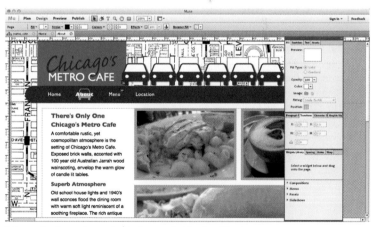

Muse displays the selected page in Design Mode.

Accessing Tools in Design Mode

Design Mode contains its own set of tools. This exclusive tool set includes the Selection, Crop, Text, Zoom, Hand, and Rectangle tools. To work with a specific tool, you must first select it by clicking its icon. The tool icons are displayed in a row at the top of the Muse interface, to the right of the Mode buttons.

Click the tool icons

1 Choose **Design Mode** from the **View** menu.

TIMESAVER *Press Cmd+L (Mac) or Ctrl+L (Win) to apply the Design Mode command quickly.*

2 Hover the mouse cursor over any of the tool icons located at the top of the Muse interface. Muse displays the tool's name in a tooltip, followed by its one-letter keyboard shortcut.

3 To select a tool, click its icon.

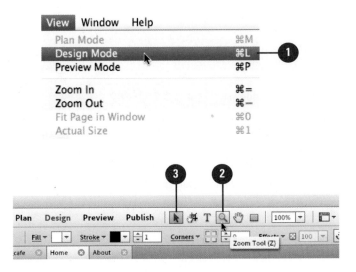

Did You Know?

You can also use keyboard shortcuts to select tools. Each tool has a one-letter keyboard shortcut assigned to it. To identify the keyboard shortcut, hover the mouse cursor over the tool's icon and refer to the tooltip that appears. The letter displayed in parentheses is what you need to press in order to access the tool.

Showing and Hiding Design Mode Panels

The Design Mode panels are essential to creating dynamic web pages in Muse. There are various panels for working with color swatches, text, assets, styles, widgets, and more. You can show and hide these panels by choosing the Hide/Show Panels command under the Window menu. All of the panels (except for the Control panel) are automatically grouped together into a vertical panel column. By selecting a specific panel from the Window menu, you can bring it to the front of the panel group.

Choose the Window panel commands

1. Choose **Design Mode** from the **View** menu.

   TIMESAVER *Press Cmd+L (Mac) or Ctrl+L (Win) to apply the Design Mode command quickly.*

2. If the vertical panel column is currently hidden, choose **Show Panels** from under the **Window** menu.

3. Choose a specific panel from the Window menu to bring it to the forefront of the panel group. Muse places a check mark next to the open panel in the Window menu list.

   IMPORTANT *The Control panel is the only panel not grouped into the vertical panel column. When visible, it appears at the top of the interface just above the web pages and below the tools.*

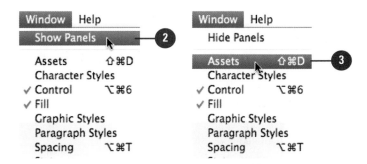

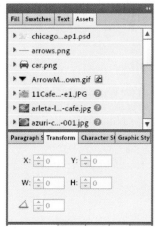

Muse brings the selected panel to the front of the group.

Did You Know?

You can also bring a panel to the front of a group by clicking its panel tab. You do not have to rely on the Window commands to bring a specific panel to the front of a panel group. You can also do so by clicking the panel's tab (where the panel's name appears).

Collapsing and Expanding Panels

The vertical panel column is a free-floating window that can be positioned anywhere onscreen. You can reposition the panels by clicking and dragging the gray bar at the top of the column. Note that Muse does not allow you to drag panels out of their groups and free-float them individually onscreen. You can, however, collapse the entire column into a thin strip of panel icons. Doing so enables you to take up less room onscreen so that you can focus on your page design. When you are ready to work with the panels again, click any panel icon and the column automatically expands.

Click the collapse/expand arrow

1. If the vertical panel column is currently hidden, choose **Show Panels** from under the **Window** menu.

2. To collapse the panels, click the left-facing arrow positioned in the upper-right corner of the vertical column.

   Muse collapses the panel column into a thin strip of panel icons.

   IMPORTANT *To identify collapsed panels, hover over each icon and refer to the name that appears in the tooltip.*

3. To expand the panels, click the right-facing arrow positioned in the upper-right corner of the vertical column.

   Muse expands the panel column to reveal all of the panel groups.

Did You Know?

You cannot dock the vertical panel column to the sides of the screen. Unlike Adobe InDesign and Dreamweaver, Muse does not allow you to dock the panel column to the sides of your screen. It must remain free-floating at all times.

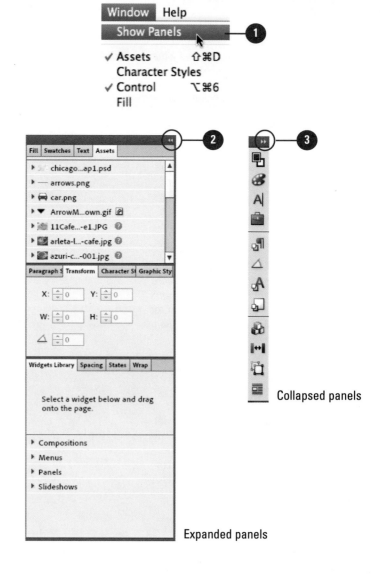

Collapsed panels

Expanded panels

Changing the View Percentage

By default, the Design Mode view percentage is set to 100%. This is the actual size of the web page when displayed in a browser. However, Muse does allow you to change the view percentage at any time as you're designing. Doing so enables you to zoom in or out of a specific page area. There are several ways to accomplish this task: by applying the Zoom command, by choosing a preset from the Zoom field, or by working with the Zoom tool.

Use the Zoom In/Zoom Out commands

1. Choose **Design Mode** from the **View** menu.

   TIMESAVER *Press Cmd+L (Mac) or Ctrl+L (Win) to apply the Design Mode command quickly.*

2. Choose **View > Zoom In** to increase the zoom percentage; choose **View > Zoom Out** to decrease it.

   TIMESAVER *Press Cmd+= (Mac) or Ctrl+= (Win) to apply the Zoom In command quickly; press Cmd+- (Mac) or Ctrl+- (Win) to apply the Zoom Out command quickly.*

   IMPORTANT *When applying the Zoom commands, Muse changes the view percentage for the current web page using 25% increments—but only up to 250%. From 250% onward, the zoom increments increase to 100%. The lowest zoom percentage you can apply using the Zoom Out command is 10%.*

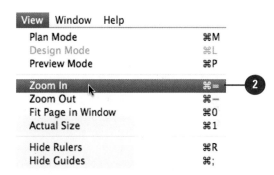

Use the Zoom percentage field

1 Choose **Design Mode** from the **View** menu.

TIMESAVER *Press Cmd+L (Mac) or Ctrl+L (Win) to apply the Design Mode command quickly.*

2 At the top of the interface, click the down-facing arrow to the right of the Zoom percentage field and choose a zoom preset, such as 50%, 75%, or 100%.

IMPORTANT *100% is the actual size the web page is displayed at in a browser.*

Did You Know?

You can also type a percentage into the Zoom field. You can apply a specific zoom percentage (such as 85%) that is not available as a preset. To do so, double-click in the Zoom percentge field to highlight the current value, and then enter the desired value.

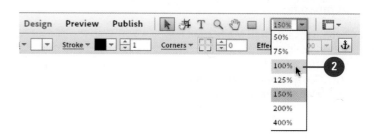

Use the Zoom tool

① Choose **Design Mode** from the **View** menu.

> **TIMESAVER** *Press Cmd+L (Mac) or Ctrl+L (Win) to apply the Design Mode command quickly.*

② At the top of the interface, click the **Zoom tool** icon.

> **TIMESAVER** *Press Z to access the Zoom tool quickly.*

③ Hover the Zoom tool cursor (the magnifying glass) over the page area you'd like to zoom into and click. Continue clicking until you reach the preferred zoom percentage.

④ To zoom out, hover the Zoom tool cursor over the page area you'd like to zoom out of and Option+click (Mac) or Alt+click (Win).

Muse displays a minus symbol in the Zoom tool cursor when you hold down the Option/Alt modifier key.

> **IMPORTANT** *When clicking with the Zoom tool, Muse changes the view percentage in 25% increments—but only up to 250%. From 250% onward, the zoom increments increase to 100%. The lowest zoom percentage you can apply using the Zoom tool is 10%.*

Did You Know?

You can also marquee over an area with the Zoom tool. To do so, click and drag over the area you'd like to zoom into and then click.

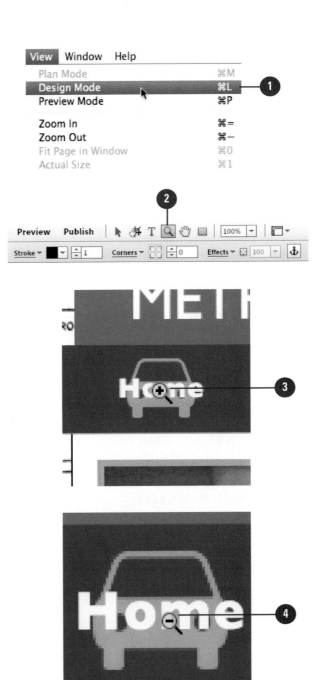

Fitting the Page in Window

The vertical page size is determined by the position of the first and fourth horizontal page guides. You can adjust the page size by repositioning these guides. By default, the Design Mode view percentage is set to 100%, which generally does not fit the entire page in the window. To fit the entire page, you must choose the Fit Page in Window command from the View menu.

Choose the Fit Page in Window command

1. Choose **Design Mode** from the **View** menu

   TIMESAVER *Press Cmd+L (Mac) or Ctrl+L (Win) to apply the Design Mode command quickly.*

2. To display the entire page in the window (not including the header), choose **Fit Page in Window** from the **View** menu.

   TIMESAVER *Press Cmd+0 (zero) (Mac) or Ctrl+0 (Win) to apply the Fit in Window command quickly.*

   Muse changes the view percentage to fit the entire page in the window.

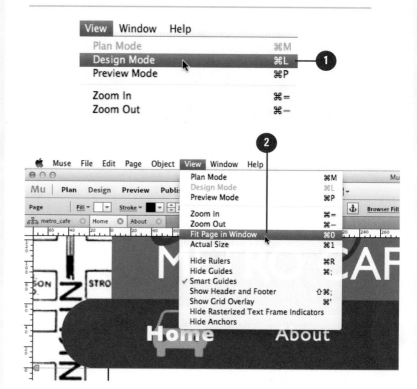

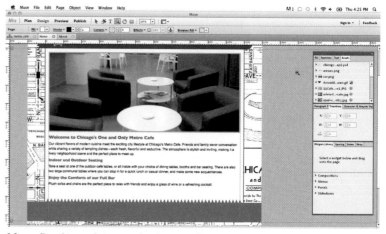

Muse fits the entire page in the window.

Viewing at Actual Size

By default, the Design Mode view percentage is set to Actual Size (100%). This is the actual size of the web page when displayed in a browser. If you should increase or decrease the view percentage while designing, you can return to actual size at any time by applying the Actual Size command.

Choose the Actual Size command

1. Choose **Design Mode** from the **View** menu.

   TIMESAVER *Press Cmd+L (Mac) or Ctrl+L (Win) to apply the Design Mode command quickly.*

2. Choose **View > Zoom In** to increase the zoom percentage; choose **View > Zoom Out** to decrease it. Continue applying the command until you reach the preferred zoom percentage.

   TIMESAVER *Press Cmd+= (Mac) or Ctrl+= (Win) to apply the Zoom In command quickly; press Cmd+- (Mac) or Ctrl+- (Win) to apply the Zoom Out command quickly.*

3. To display the page at actual size (100%), choose **Actual Size** from the **View** menu.

   TIMESAVER *Press Cmd+1 (Mac) or Ctrl+1 (Win) to apply the Actual Size command quickly.*

   Muse changes the view percentage to display the page at actual size.

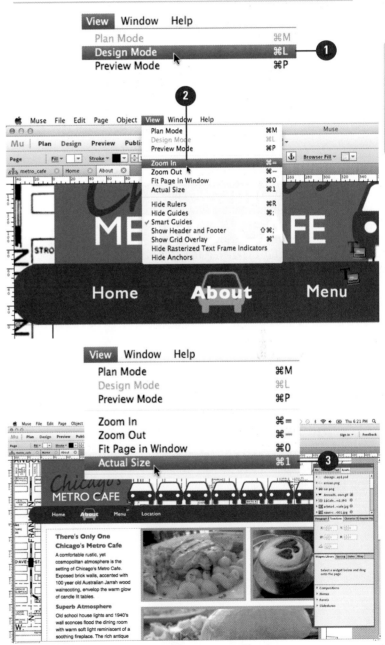

Muse displays the page at 100% view magnification.

Showing and Hiding Rulers

You can use the Design Mode rulers to help position and align page objects, such as buttons, photos, and links. The horizontal ruler appears above the web pages, while the vertical ruler appears to the left of them. Each ruler displays pixels as the default unit of measurement (there is currently no preference for changing ruler measurement units). You can hide and show the rulers by applying the Show/Hide Rulers commands.

Choose the Show/Hide Rulers command

① Choose **Design Mode** from the **View** menu.

TIMESAVER *Press Cmd+L (Mac) or Ctrl+L (Win) to apply the Design Mode command quickly.*

② To make the rulers visible, choose **Show Rulers** from the **View** menu.

TIMESAVER *Press Cmd+R (Mac) or Ctrl+R (Win) to apply the Show/Hide Rulers command quickly.*

Muse displays the horizontal ruler above the web page and the vertical ruler to the left of the web page.

③ To hide the rulers, choose **Hide Rulers** from the **View** menu.

Did You Know?

You can also choose the Show/Hide Rulers command from the contextual menu. To do so, right-click or Control-click (Mac) in the ruler area (Hide Rulers) or anywhere on the web page (Show Rulers and Hide Rulers).

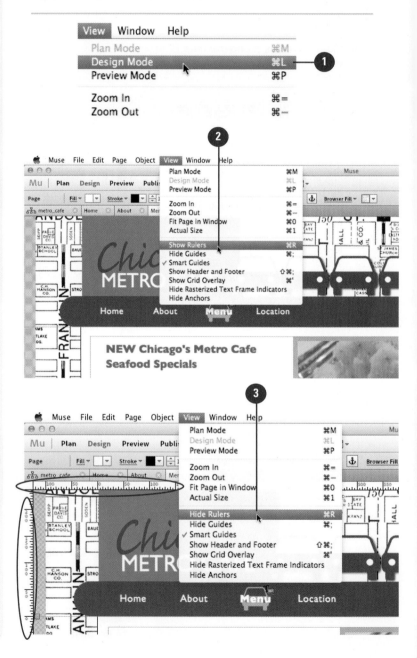

Showing and Hiding Page Guides

The first, fourth, and fifth horizontal guides on the page are referred to as page guides. You can drag the first guide up or the fourth guide down to extend the content area of the page. The fifth guide indicates the bottom of the browser. Note that unlike InDesign, there are no vertical page rulers, and you cannot drag additional page rulers out from the vertical or horizontal rulers. After the content area is set, you can hide the page guides by choosing the Hide Guides command.

Choose the Show/Hide Guides command

1 Choose **Design Mode** from the **View** menu.

> **TIMESAVER** *Press Cmd+L (Mac) or Ctrl+L (Win) to apply the Design Mode command quickly.*

2 To make the guides visible, choose **Show Guides** from the **View** menu.

> **TIMESAVER** *Press Cmd+; (semicolon) (Mac) or Ctrl+; (Win) to apply the Show/Hide Guides command quickly.*

Muse displays the page guides in blue, each with a left-facing blue arrow next to the vertical ruler.

3 To hide the guides, choose **Hide Guides** from the **View** menu.

Did You Know?

You can also choose the Show/Hide Guides command from the contextual menu. To do so, right-click or Control-click (Mac) in the ruler area or anywhere on the web page.

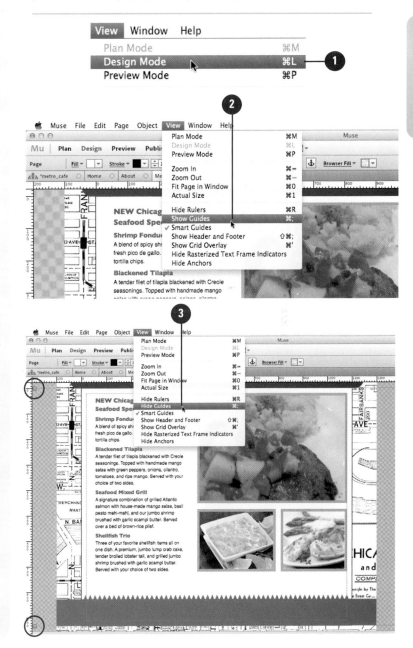

Showing and Hiding Header and Footer Guides

The second and third guides on the page are referred to as header and footer guides. You can drag the second guide to determine the height of the header area. Drag the third guide to determine the height of the footer area. After these areas are set, you can hide these two guides by choosing the Hide Header and Footer command.

Choose the Show/Hide Header and Footer command

1. Choose **Design Mode** from the **View** menu.

   TIMESAVER *Press Cmd+L (Mac) or Ctrl+L (Win) to apply the Design Mode command quickly.*

2. To make the header and footer guides visible, choose **Show Header and Footer** from the **View** menu.

   TIMESAVER *Press Shift+Cmd+; (semicolon) (Mac) or Shift+Ctrl+; (Win) to apply the Show/Hide Header and Footer command quickly.*

3. To hide the header and footer guides, choose **Hide Header and Footer** from the **View** menu.

Did You Know?

You can also choose the Show/Hide Header and Footer command from the contextual menu. To do so, right-click or Control-click (Mac) in the ruler area or anywhere on the web page.

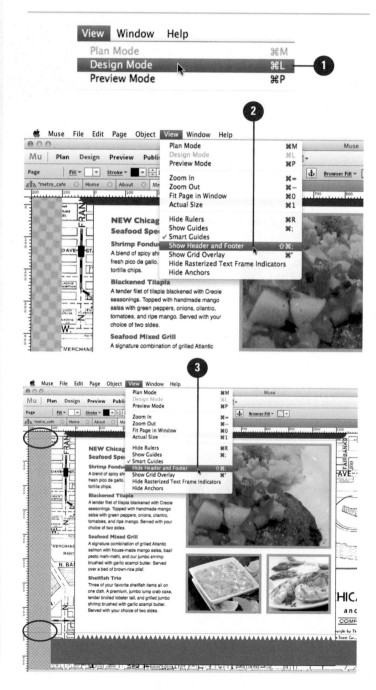

Showing and Hiding Smart Guides

Smart guides can be used in conjunction with the rulers to position and align multiple page objects. As you reposition selected objects on the page, the smart guides automatically appear to let you know when the objects are aligned with others nearby. You can show and hide the smart guides by applying the Smart Guides command.

Choose the Smart Guides command

1 Choose **Design Mode** from the **View** menu.

> **TIMESAVER** *Press Cmd+L (Mac) or Ctrl+L (Win) to apply the Design Mode command quickly.*

2 To make smart guides visible, choose **Smart Guides** from the **View** menu. Muse places a check mark next to the command in the menu.

3 Click the **Selection Tool** icon at the top of the interface.

> **TIMESAVER** *Press V to access the Selection tool quickly.*

4 Click and drag any object on the page.

Muse displays smart guides when the selected object becomes aligned with another object nearby.

5 To hide smart guides, choose **Smart Guides** from the **View** menu. Muse removes the check mark that was next to the command in the menu.

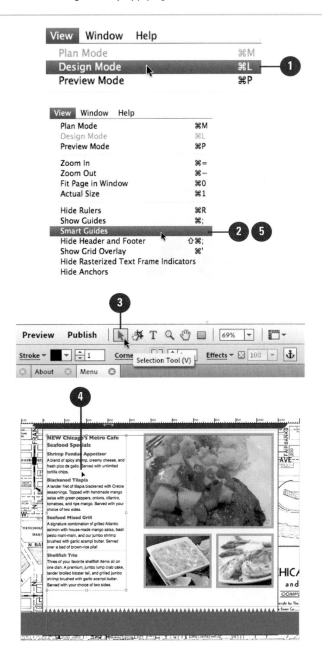

Showing and Hiding the Grid Overlay

If you are ever unsure what the active design area is for the current web page, you can highlight it by turning on the grid overlay. When you do, Muse displays a light pink box (not a grid pattern) over the active areas of the page, not the header area or background. This is the area determined by the position of the first and fourth horizontal page guides. You can adjust the overall page size by repositioning these guides.

Choose the Show/Hide Grid Overlay command

1. Choose **Design Mode** from the **View** menu.

   TIMESAVER *Press Cmd+L (Mac) or Ctrl+L (Win) to apply the Design Mode command quickly.*

2. To make the grid overlay visible, choose **Show Grid Overlay** from the **View** menu.

   TIMESAVER *Press Cmd+' (apostrophe) (Mac) or Ctrl+' (Win) to apply the Show/Hide Grid Overlay command quickly.*

3. To hide the grid overlay, choose **Hide Grid Overlay** from the **View** menu.

Did You Know?

You can also choose the Show/Hide Grid Overlay command from the contextual menu. To do so, right-click or Control-click (Mac) in the ruler area or anywhere on the web page.

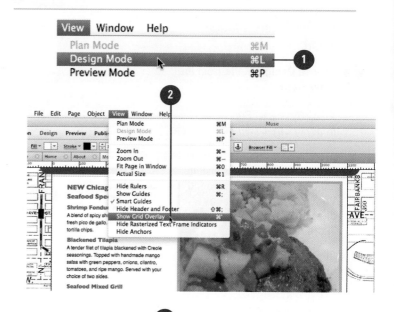

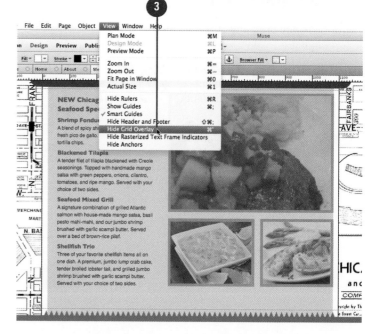

Creating and Planning a Website

3

Introduction

After you've spent some time becoming familiar with the Muse work environment, the next step is to create a new website from scratch. Thankfully, by utilizing the sitemap features available in Plan Mode, creating and planning a new website has never been easier.

With this chapter, you'll learn how to use the New Site dialog box to specify the page size for your new site, as well as the placement of margin and column guides and the amount of padding to leave between the pages and the edges of the browser. After you create a new site document, you'll learn how to add, rearrange, and delete pages—all by working with the sitemap page thumbnails in Plan Mode.

This chapter also shows you how to create and apply master pages. By utilizing master pages, you can ensure that any repeating page elements, such as nav bars and footers, maintain their position throughout your site. This is achieved by placing the repeating elements on a master page, and then applying the master page to site pages.

Additionally, you'll learn how to fill the browser with a background color or image and set objects to display at 100% browser width. The final sections of the chapter explain how to save and close your website projects.

Creating a New Site

When you create a new site in Muse, you must indicate what page dimensions you'd like to use, as well as where to place the margin and column guides. This is done by entering values in the New Site dialog box, which appears whenever you choose New Site from the File menu, or by clicking the New Site button in the Welcome Screen. The entire process is similar to creating a new page in InDesign.

Use the Welcome Screen

1. Launch Muse, as described in Chapter 1 "Getting Started with Adobe Muse." This process varies depending on what platform you are on (Mac OS X or Windows).

   By default, the Welcome Screen automatically appears.

2. Click the **Create New Site** button in the upper left of the Welcome Screen.

   Muse displays the New Site dialog box.

3. Enter the preferred pixel dimensions in the **Page Width** and **Min Height** fields. Generally, 1280 width by 1024 height is considered a standard size.

4. To center the web pages horizontally in the browser window, place a check in the **Center Horizontally** checkbox.

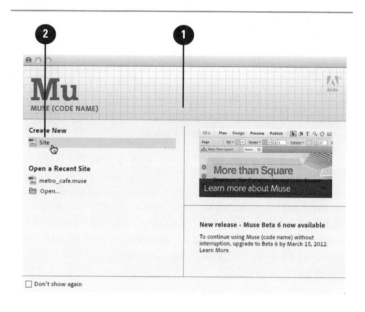

See Also

See Chapter 1, "Getting Started with Adobe Muse," to learn more about launching the application and accessing the Welcome Screen.

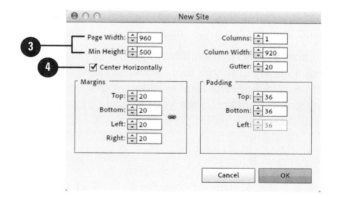

5 Enter the preferred values in the **Columns**, **Column Width**, and **Gutter** fields. These values determine where the column guides are positioned on the pages.

6 Enter the preferred values in the **Top**, **Bottom**, **Left**, and **Right Margins** fields. These values determine the amount of space surrounding the content on each page, as indicated by the margin guides.

7 Enter values in the **Top**, **Bottom**, and **Left Padding** fields to determine the amount of space placed between the web pages and the edges of the web browser.

IMPORTANT *When you enable the Center Horizontally option (see Step 4), you cannot enter a value in the Left Padding field. The option appears "grayed out" in the dialog box. This is because the padding between your page and the left edge of the browser will change automatically depending on the size of the browser window.*

8 Click **OK** to apply the New Site settings.

Muse displays the new site in Plan Mode.

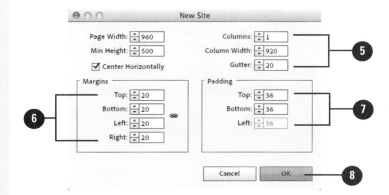

Did You Know?

You can change these site settings at any time via the Site Properties dialog box. To do so, choose Site Properties from the File menu. Enter the new page dimensions, margin and column guide settings, and padding settings and click OK to apply them to your site.

Choose the New Site command

① Choose **New Site** from the **File** menu.

TIMESAVER *Press Cmd+N (Mac) or Ctrl+N (Win) to apply the New Site command quickly.*

Muse displays the New Site dialog box.

② Enter the preferred pixel dimensions in the **Page Width** and **Min Height** fields.

③ To center the web pages horizontally in the browser window, place a check in the **Center Horizontally** checkbox.

④ Enter the preferred values in the **Columns**, **Column Width**, and **Gutter** fields. These values determine where the column guides are positioned on the pages.

⑤ Enter the preferred values in the **Top**, **Bottom**, **Left**, and **Right Margins** fields. These values determine the amount of space surrounding the content on each page, as indicated by the margin guides.

⑥ Enter values in the **Top**, **Bottom**, and **Left Padding** fields to determine the amount of space placed between the web pages and the edges of the web browser.

IMPORTANT *When you enable the Center Horizontally option (see Step 3), you cannot enter a value in the Left Padding field. The option appears "grayed out" in the dialog box.*

⑦ Click **OK** to apply the New Site settings.

Muse displays the new site in Plan Mode.

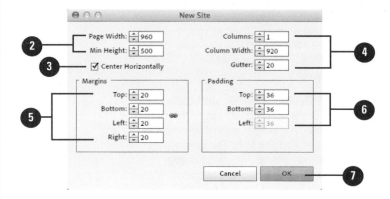

Adding Top Level (Sibling) Pages to the Sitemap

In Plan Mode, you can use the sitemap to create the page structure and hierarchy for your website. When you add pages, you are not only adding them to the sitemap, but also to the site itself. By double-clicking the page thumbnails in the sitemap, you can open them up in Design Mode and add page contents. You can add pages by choosing the Add New Top Level Page command from the Page menu, or by clicking the Insert Page buttons.

Choose the Add New Top Level Page command

① If you're not already in Plan Mode, choose **Plan Mode** from the **View** menu.

TIMESAVER *Press Cmd+M (Mac) or Ctrl+M (Win) to apply the Plan Mode command quickly.*

② Choose **Add New Top Level Page** from the **Page** menu.

TIMESAVER *Press Cmd+Shift+P (Mac) or Ctrl+Shift+P (Win) to apply the Add New Top Level Page command quickly.*

Muse adds the page to the site. The new page thumbnail appears to the right of the last page in the sitemap. Muse highlights the page name so that you can enter a new one.

③ Enter a name for the new page and press **Return** (Mac) or **Enter** (Win) to apply it.

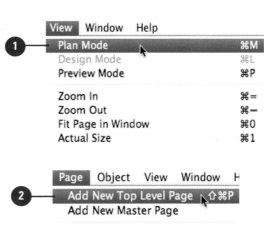

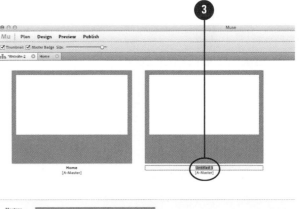

Click the Insert Page buttons

1. Choose **Plan Mode** from the **View** menu.

   TIMESAVER *Press Cmd+M (Mac) or Ctrl+M (Win) to apply the Plan Mode command quickly.*

2. Hover the cursor over any page in the sitemap and click the **Insert Page** button (the plus icon) that appears to the left or right of the thumbnail.

   Muse adds the page to the site. The new page thumbnail appears to the left or right of whichever button you clicked. Muse highlights the page name so that you can enter a new one.

3. Enter a name for the new page and press **Return** (Mac) or **Enter** (Win) to apply it.

Did You Know?

You can also insert top level (sibling) pages using the contextual menu. To do so, right-click or Control-click (Mac) on any page in the sitemap and choose New Sibling Page from the contextual menu. The new page thumbnail appears to the right of the page you clicked.

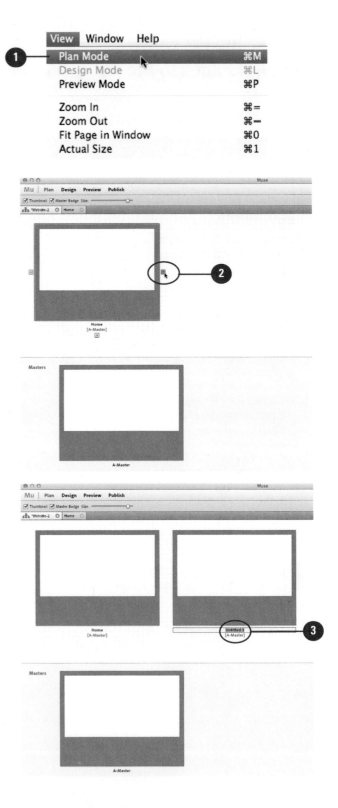

Adding Child Pages to the Sitemap

End users generally visit a child page by accessing its parent page first. Because of this, child pages do not appear in the top level navigation bar, but rather in a drop-down menu via the top level parent page. Muse even generates and updates nav bars automatically as you add, remove, and rearrange pages in the sitemap (see Chapter 4, "Adding Navigational Content"). You can add child pages by clicking the Insert Child Page button.

Click the Insert Child Page button

1. Choose **Plan Mode** from the **View** menu.

   TIMESAVER *Press Cmd+M (Mac) or Ctrl+M (Win) to apply the Plan Mode command quickly.*

2. Hover the cursor over any page in the sitemap and click the **Insert Child Page** button (the plus icon) that appears underneath the thumbnail.

   Muse adds the page to the site. The new page thumbnail appears underneath the button you clicked. Muse highlights the page name so that you can enter a new one.

3. Enter a name for the new page and press **Return** (Mac) or **Enter** (Win) to apply it.

Did You Know?

You can also insert child pages using the contextual menu. To do so, right-click or Control-click (Mac) on any page in the sitemap and choose New Child Page from the contextual menu. The new page thumbnail appears underneath the button you clicked.

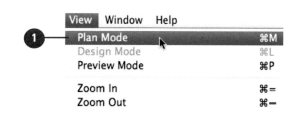

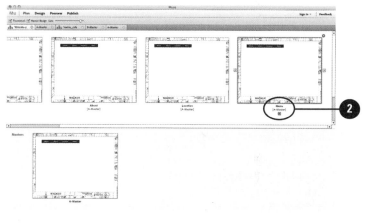

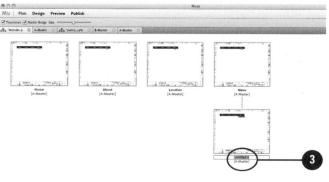

Adding Master Pages to the Sitemap

With master pages, you can ensure that any repeating page elements, such as nav bars and footers, maintain their position throughout your site. This is because master page contents only appear on the pages where the master is applied—these contents can only be edited from the master page itself. You can access master pages from the bottom portion of the Plan Mode window. Every new site you create contains a single, editable master page, but you can add as many master pages as you like.

Choose the Add New Master Page command

① Choose **Plan Mode** from the **View** menu.

> **TIMESAVER** *Press Cmd+M (Mac) or Ctrl+M (Win) to apply the Plan Mode command quickly.*

② Choose **Add New Master Page** from the **Page** menu.

Muse adds the page to the site. The new page thumbnail appears to the right of the last page in the sitemap. Muse highlights the page name so that you can enter a new one.

③ Enter a name for the new master page and press **Return** (Mac) or **Enter** (Win) to apply it.

Did You Know?

You can also insert master pages using the contextual menu. To do so, right-click or Control-click (Mac) on a master page from the Masters section of the sitemap and choose New Master Page from the contextual menu.

Click the Insert Master Page buttons

1 Choose **Plan Mode** from the **View** menu.

TIMESAVER *Press Cmd+M (Mac) or Ctrl+M (Win) to apply the Plan Mode command quickly.*

2 Hover the cursor over any master page in the Masters portion of the sitemap and click the **Insert Page** button (the plus icon) that appears to the left or right of the thumbnail.

Muse adds the master page to the site. The new master page thumbnail appears to the left or right of whichever button you clicked. Muse highlights the master page name so that you can enter a new one.

3 Enter a name for the new master page and press **Return** (Mac) or **Enter** (Win) to apply it.

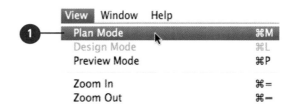

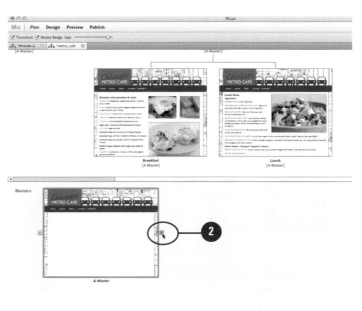

Removing Pages from the Sitemap

Removing pages from a site is just as easy as adding them. All you need to do is hover the mouse cursor over the page thumbnail in the sitemap and click the Delete Page button that appears. Muse instantly removes the page from the site and also removes it automatically from any navigational content (see Chapter 4, "Adding Navigational Content").

Click the Delete Page button

1. Choose **Plan Mode** from the **View** menu.

   TIMESAVER *Press Cmd+M (Mac) or Ctrl+M (Win) to apply the Plan Mode command quickly.*

2. Hover the cursor over any page or master page in the sitemap.

   The Delete Page button (the x icon) appears in the upper-right corner, above the page thumbnail.

3. Click the **Delete Page** button.

   If the page contains contents (other than master page contents), then Muse displays the Delete Page warning dialog box.

4. Click **OK** to delete the page.

   Muse removes the page from the site.

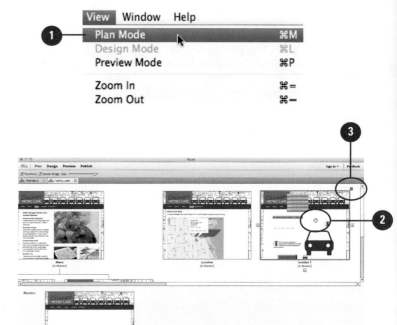

Did You Know?

You can also delete pages using the contextual menu. To do so, right-click or Control-click (Mac) on any page or master page in the sitemap and choose Delete Page from the contextual menu.

Rearranging Pages in the Sitemap

With Muse, changing the page order of your website has never been easier. By clicking and dragging the page thumbnails in the Plan Mode sitemap, you can easily rearrange the site structure and page hierarchy for a site. If the Include Page in Navigation feature is enabled (Muse enables this by default), then the new site structure and hierarchy are automatically updated in the site's nav bars (see Chapter 4, "Adding Navigational Content").

Click and drag the page thumbnail

1. Choose **Plan Mode** from the **View** menu.

   TIMESAVER *Press Cmd+M (Mac) or Ctrl+M (Win) to apply the Plan Mode command quickly.*

2. Hover the cursor over any page or master page in the sitemap. Click and drag the thumbnail to move the page to a new location in the sitemap.

   To place the page between two existing pages, drag the thumbnail between page thumbnails until the blue rectangle appears, and then release the mouse button.

3. To place the page under an existing page and convert it into a child page, drag the thumbnail over the parent thumbnail until the blue rectangle appears underneath it, and then release the mouse button.

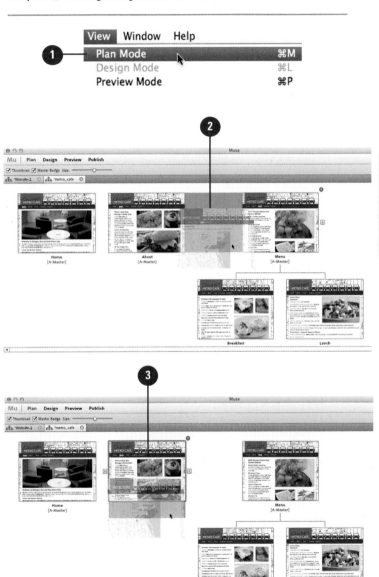

Resizing Sitemap Thumbnails

As you add more and more pages to a website, the Plan Mode sitemap can fill up quickly with thumbnails. In order to view all of the thumbnails at once in the window, you must decrease their size. However, with all of the thumbnails visible, it may become too difficult to see the page names. When this happens, you must increase their size. Thankfully, you can change the size of the sitemap thumbnails in one of two ways: by dragging the Size slider at the top of the interface, or by choosing the Zoom commands from the View menu.

Drag the Size slider

1. Choose **Plan Mode** from the **View** menu.

    TIMESAVER *Press Cmd+M (Mac) or Ctrl+M (Win) to apply the Plan Mode command quickly.*

2. Drag the **Size** slider to the left to decrease the size of all the thumbnails in the sitemap, including master pages.

    Muse displays the thumbnails at the new size in the Plan Mode window.

3. Drag the **Size** slider to the right to increase the size of all the thumbnails in the sitemap, including master pages.

    Muse displays the thumbnails at the new size in the Plan Mode window.

Did You Know?

You can hide thumbnail previews. By default, the thumbnail preview option is enabled. This option displays a preview of each page inside the sitemap thumbnails. While this can be a useful feature for helping to identify the pages you want to work with, it can also slow down your workflow, especially when working with sites that contain a large number of pages. To disable the preview fature, uncheck the Thumbnail option located in the upper left of the interface.

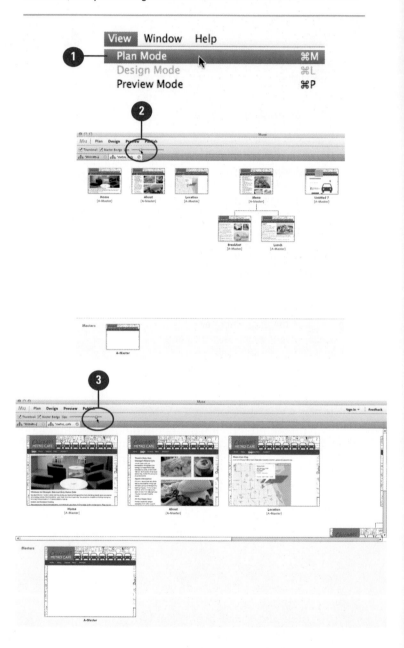

Choose the Zoom In/Zoom Out commands

1 Choose **Plan Mode** from the **View** menu.

> **TIMESAVER** *Press Cmd+M (Mac) or Ctrl+M (Win) to apply the Plan Mode command quickly.*

2 Choose **View > Zoom In** to increase the thumbnail size; choose **View > Zoom Out** to decrease it.

> **TIMESAVER** *Press Cmd+= (Mac) or Ctrl+= (Win) to apply the Zoom In command quickly; press Cmd+- (Mac) or Ctrl+- (Win) to apply the Zoom Out command quickly.*

Muse displays the thumbnails at the new size in the Plan Mode window.

View	Window	Help
Plan Mode		⌘M
Design Mode		⌘L
Preview Mode		⌘P
Zoom In		⌘=
Zoom Out		⌘-
Fit Page in Window		⌘0
Actual Size		⌘1
Hide Rulers		⌘R
Hide Guides		⌘;
✓ Smart Guides		
Hide Header and Footer		⇧⌘;
Show Grid Overlay		⌘'
Hide Rasterized Text Frame Indicators		
Hide Anchors		

View	Window	Help
Plan Mode		⌘M
Design Mode		⌘L
Preview Mode		⌘P
Zoom In		⌘=
Zoom Out		⌘-
Fit Page in Window		⌘0
Actual Size		⌘1
Hide Rulers		⌘R
Hide Guides		⌘;
✓ Smart Guides		
Hide Header and Footer		⇧⌘;
Show Grid Overlay		⌘'
Hide Rasterized Text Frame Indicators		
Hide Anchors		

Filling the Browser with a Background Color

One way to maintain consistent color throughout your site is to fill the browser window with the same background color that you're using on your web pages. You can achieve this effect in Muse by using the Browser Fill feature. To make it even easier, you can use the Browser Fill feature on a master page and apply the master to all of your web pages. You can choose colors to work with using a traditional Color Picker, very similar to what you would use in other Adobe products, such as InDesign, Photoshop, or Illustator.

Use the Browser Fill Color option

1. In Plan Mode, double-click a new page or master page thumbnail from the sitemap.

   Muse opens the page in Design Mode.

2. Click the **Browser Fill Color** swatch in the **Control** panel.

   Muse displays a drop-down Color Picker.

3. Choose a background color with the Color Picker via any of the following methods:

   ◆ Enter values into the **RGB** fields.

   ◆ Enter a hexadecimal code in the **Hex#** field.

   ◆ Click a **swatch** from the saved **color swatch list**.

   ◆ Drag the **Hue** slider up or down to select a color hue. Then click in the color field to the right of the Hue slider to determine the saturation and brightness of the selected color.

   ◆ Click the **Sample Color** tool icon. To sample a color for the background, proceed to click anywhere on the page—including in a placed photo or graphic.

   Muse fills the browser with the chosen background color.

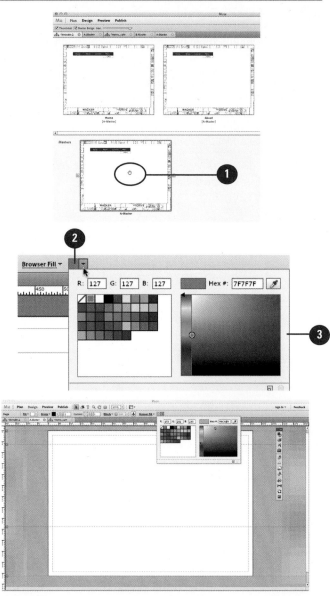

Muse fills the browser with the chosen background color.

Filling the Browser with a Background Image

In web design it's very common to fill the browser window with a tiled background graphic. By doing so, the background graphics repeat endelssly whenever you enlarge the browser window. You can also incorporate tiled graphics into your overall site design by placing page contents, such as nav bars, text, or photos, over them. One of the best ways to utilize tiled graphics is to fill the browser with them on your master pages. You can also fill a rectangle with tiled graphics and place them as page contents or as footers (see Chapter 5, "Working with Graphics").

Use the Browser Fill Image option

1. In Plan Mode, double-click a new page or master page thumbnail from the sitemap.

   Muse opens the page in Design Mode.

2. Click the **Browser Fill** button in the **Control** panel.

   Muse displays a drop-down Fill panel.

3. Click the **Choose Background Image** button (the folder icon).

   Muse displays the Import dialog box.

4. Using the Import dialog box, navigate to the background image on your system disk. Click the image file to select it and then click **Select**.

   IMPORTANT *You can only import images saved in the following file formats: PNG, PSD, JPEG, and GIF.*

   Muse fills the browser with the chosen background image.

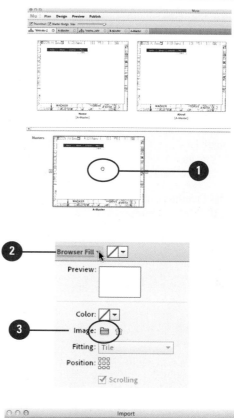

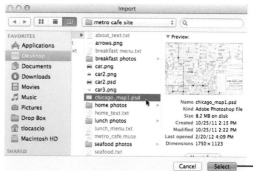

5 Choose a fitting option from the **Fitting** drop-down list. Options include: **Original Size, Tile, Tile Horizontally,** and **Tile Vertically**.

> **IMPORTANT** *The Tile options enable you to repeat the image in the brower background. The Tile option repeats the image both horizontally and vertically.*

6 Click one of the small squares next to the **Position** option in the Fill drop-down panel. By doing so, you can determine where the image starts repeating from in the browser window.

7 Enable the **Scrolling** option to allow tiled background graphics (that do not fill the entire browser window) to move with the rest of the page contents when scrolling.

Disable the **Scrolling** option if you'd like the tiled background graphics to remain fixed in position as you scroll the page in a browser.

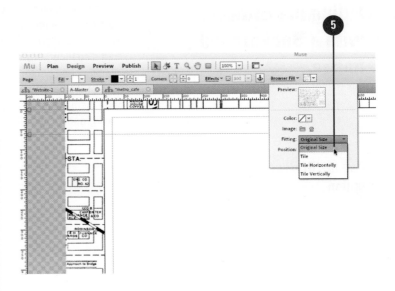

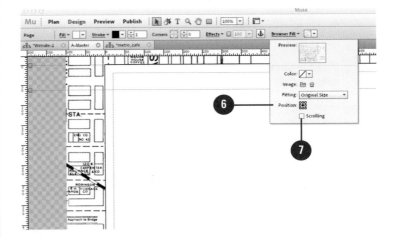

Applying Master Pages

When you apply a master page, all master page contents are applied to a site page and can only be edited from the master. By default, whenever you create a new site, the A-master page is automatically applied to the intial web page and any additional pages you add. However, when you create additional master pages in Plan Mode, you can apply them to your site pages by dragging-and-dropping the master page thumbnail over the page thumbnail in the sitemap. You can also change the master page that is currently applied to a site page by choosing a diferent master from the contextual menu.

Drag-and-drop the master page thumbnail

1. Choose **Plan Mode** from the **View** menu.

   TIMESAVER *Press Cmd+M (Mac) or Ctrl+M (Win) to apply the Plan Mode command quickly.*

2. Click and drag the master page thumbnail over the site page thumbnail in the sitemap.

   Muse displays a blue rectangle around the site page thumbnail.

3. Release the mouse button to apply the master page to the site page.

   Muse adds the master page contents to the site page.

Did You Know?

You can hide master badges. By default, the name of the applied master page appears underneath the thumbnail for each page in the sitemap. To hide the master badge, uncheck the Master Badge option located in the upper-left corner of the interface.

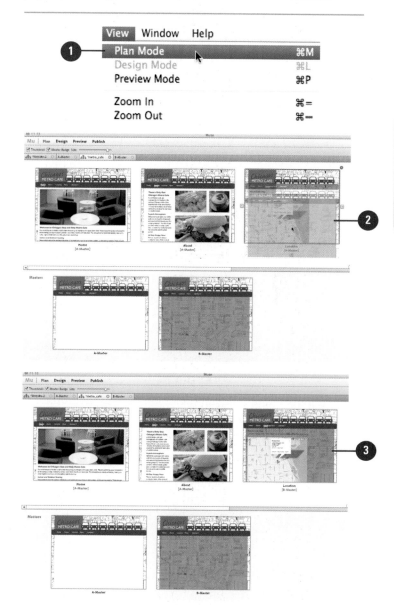

Choose a master page from the contextual menu

1 Choose **Plan Mode** from the **View** menu.

TIMESAVER *Press Cmd+M (Mac) or Ctrl+M (Win) to apply the Plan Mode command quickly.*

2 Right-click or Control-click (Mac) on any page in the sitemap to access the contextual menu. Choose the master page from the Masters submenu.

Muse adds the master page contents to the site page.

Did You Know?

You can also apply no master page at all. To do so, right-click or Control-click (Mac) on any page in the sitemap to access the contextual menu. Choose No Master from the Masters submenu. Muse removes all master page contents from the page.

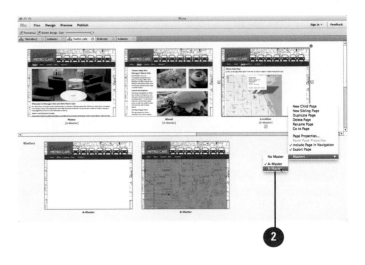

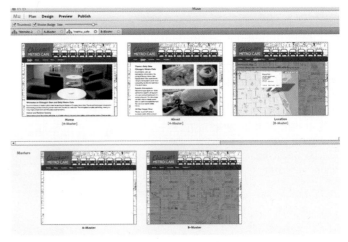

Muse adds the master page contents to the chosen site page.

Saving a Site

As it is when working with any design software, it's always a good idea to save often. With Muse, you can save your website projects at any time, no matter whether you are working in Plan Mode, Design Mode, or Preview Mode. To do so, choose Save Site from the File menu. When you do, Muse saves all of the data for the entire site, including all pages, master pages, and their respective contents. To create a copy of a site, or create a different version of it, choose Save Site As.

Choose Save Site

1. Choose **Save Site** from the **File** menu.

   TIMESAVER *Press Cmd+S (Mac) or Ctrl+S (Win) to apply the Save Site command quickly.*

   IMPORTANT *You can choose the Save Site command from the File menu at any time, while working in any of the three modes (Plan, Design, or Preview).*

   IMPORTANT *When saving a site for the first time, Muse displays the Save Muse File As dialog box. You can use this dialog box to name the file and choose a save location for it on your system.*

Choose Save Site As

1. Choose **Save Site As** from the **File** menu.

   TIMESAVER *Press Shift+Cmd+S (Mac) or Shift+Ctrl+S (Win) to apply the Save Site As command quickly.*

   IMPORTANT *You can choose the Save Site As command from the File menu at any time, while working in any of the three modes (Plan, Design, or Preview).*

   Muse displays the Save Muse File As dialog box.

2. Using the Save Muse As dialog box, navigate to a save location on your system disk and then click **Save**.

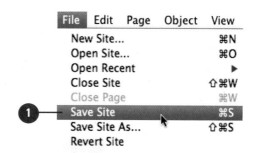

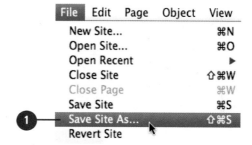

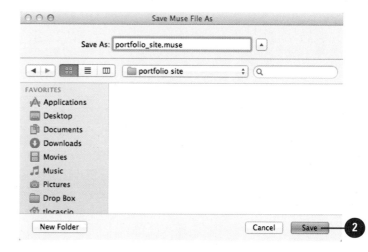

Closing a Site

Just as it is with saving sites in Muse, you can also close your website projects at any time, no matter whether you are working in Plan Mode, Design Mode, or Preview Mode. To do so, choose Close Site from the File menu. When you do, Muse closes all of the pages for the entire site, including the sitemap.

Choose the Close Site command

1. Choose **Close Site** from the **File** menu.

    TIMESAVER *Press Shift+Cmd+W (Mac) or Shift+Ctrl+W (Win) to apply the Close Site command quickly.*

    IMPORTANT *You can choose the Close Site command from the File menu at any time, while working in any of the three modes (Plan, Design, or Preview).*

2. If the site contains any unsaved changes, Muse displays the Unsaved Changes warning dialog box. To save changes before closing the site, click **Save**. To close the site without saving any changes, click **Don't Save**.

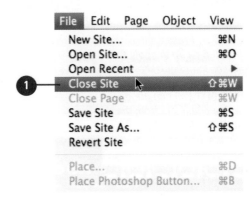

Adding Navigational Content

4

Introduction

After you've created a new site document and planned out the page structure and hierarchy using the sitemap, the next step is to add navigation to your master pages. Nav bars are traditionally found at the top of your pages in either horizontal or vertical format. Nav links can also be found in the footer area for pages that are exceptionally long.

Before you can add navigational content, you must first indicate how much space to apply as a header or footer on your pages. This chapter shows you how to use the Header and Footer guides to do just that.

In this chapter, you'll also learn how to utilize menu widgets. These are prebuilt menus that synchronize with the sitemap. As you add, delete, rearrange, or rename pages with the sitemap, the nav bars automatically apply the current edits.

Menu widgets are also entirely editable. With Muse, you can change the widget menu fill colors, text attributes, spacing, and rollover states, all without ever having to look at any code. The final sections of this chapter show you how to customize menu widgets to match your site's design.

Creating a Header

With Muse, you can determine the height of your website's header area (the area at the very top of your pages) by simply dragging a guide. The best place to do this is on a master page, so that you can ensure the header area is consistent throughout your site. Any text, graphics, or navigational elements that you place in the master page header area (above the Header guide) also appear on the site pages, wherever the master is applied.

Drag the Header guide up or down

1. Choose **Plan Mode** from the **View** menu.

   TIMESAVER *Press Cmd+M (Mac) or Ctrl+M (Win) to apply the Plan Mode command quickly.*

2. Double-click a master page thumbnail from the sitemap.

   Muse opens the master page in Design Mode.

3. Drag the **Header guide** up or down (by default this is the second guide from the top of the window). Doing so determines the height of the header area that appears on every page where the master is applied.

See Also

See Chapter 2, "Working with the Muse Environment," to learn how to show and hide Header and Footer guides.

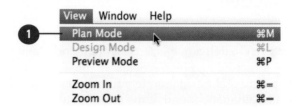

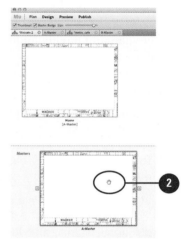

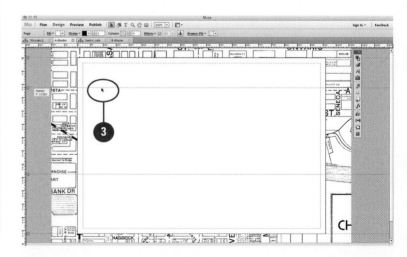

Creating a Footer

By dragging the Footer guide, you can determine the height of your website's footer area (the area at the very bottom of your pages). As it is when working with headers, the best place to set up a footer is on a master page. By doing so, you can ensure that the footers are consistent throughout your site. Any text, graphics, or navigational elements that you place in the master page footer area (below the Footer guide) also appear on the site pages, wherever the master is applied.

Drag the Footer guide up or down

1 Choose **Plan Mode** from the **View** menu.

TIMESAVER *Press Cmd+M (Mac) or Ctrl+M (Win) to apply the Plan Mode command quickly.*

2 Double-click a master page thumbnail from the sitemap.

Muse opens the master page in Design Mode.

3 Drag the **Footer guide** up or down (by default this is the third guide from the top of the window). Doing so determines the height of the footer area that appears on every page where the master is applied.

See Also

See Chapter 2, "Working with the Muse Environment," to learn how to show and hide Header and Footer guides.

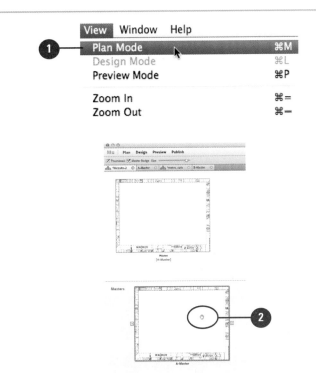

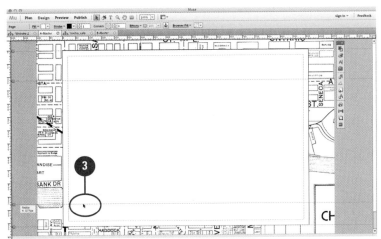

Setting Up a Horizontal Menu

The Horizontal Menu widget is a basic, no-frills menu that you can easily edit to match your site's design. The page names from the Plan Mode sitemap are automatically added—in order—to the horizontal menu using black sans-serif text and no fills. The later sections of this chapter explain how to edit the menu's appearance. For now, you can start out by inserting a Horizontal Menu widget onto a master page. To do so, drag-and-drop the Horizontal Menu widget from the Widgets Library panel.

Drag-and-drop the Horizontal Menu widget

1. Choose **Plan Mode** from the **View** menu.

   TIMESAVER *Press Cmd+M (Mac) or Ctrl+M (Win) to apply the Plan Mode command quickly.*

2. Double-click a master page thumbnail from the sitemap.

   Muse opens the master page in Design Mode.

3. If it's not visible already, choose **Window > Widgets Library** to display the Widgets Library panel.

4. Click the right-facing arrow next to **Menus** in the **Widgets Library** panel.

   Muse displays the available widget menu options, including **Bar**, **Horizontal**, and **Vertical**.

5. Click and drag the **Horizontal** menu from the **Widgets Library** panel onto the header area of the master page.

   IMPORTANT *By default, the Include Page in Navigation option is enabled for each page in the sitemap. As a result, all of the pages in the sitemap automatically appear in the widget menu when you drag it onto the page. Also, any edits you make to the pages in the sitemap (rearranging, renaming, deleting) automatically update in the menu.*

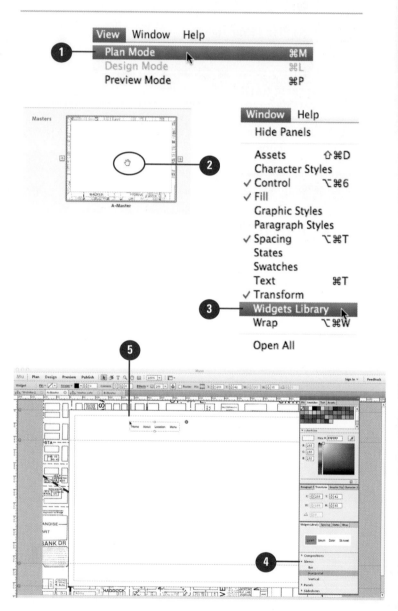

Setting Up a Bar Menu

The Bar Menu widget is very similar to the Horizontal Menu widget. They are both set up horizontally with sans-serif text. The only real difference between the two is that the Bar Menu includes gradient fills and white text in each menu button, whereas the Horizontal Menu includes black text and no fills. You can insert a Bar Menu widget by dragging-and-dropping one from the Widgets Library panel onto a master page.

Drag-and-drop the Bar Menu widget

1 Choose **Plan Mode** from the **View** menu.

> **TIMESAVER** *Press Cmd+M (Mac) or Ctrl+M (Win) to apply the Plan Mode command quickly.*

2 Double-click a master page thumbnail from the sitemap.

Muse opens the master page in Design Mode.

3 If it's not visible already, choose **Window > Widgets Library** to display the Widgets Library panel.

4 Click the right-facing arrow next to **Menus** in the **Widgets Library** panel.

Muse displays the available widget menu options, including **Bar**, **Horizontal**, and **Vertical**.

5 Click and drag the **Bar** menu from the **Widgets Library** panel onto the header area of the master page.

> **IMPORTANT** *By default, the Include Page in Navigation option is enabled for each page in the sitemap. As a result, all of the pages in the sitemap automatically appear in the widget menu when you drag it onto the page. Also, any edits you make to the pages in the sitemap (rearranging, renaming, deleting) automatically update in the menu.*

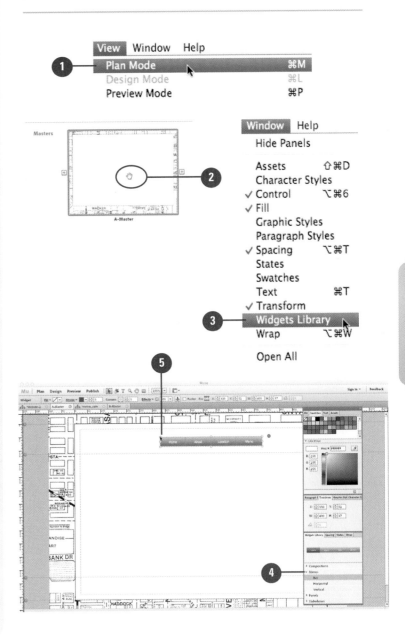

Setting Up a Vertical Menu

The Vertical Menu widget is similar in appearance to the Bar Menu widget, except in vertical format. The Vertical Menu includes gradient fills and white sans-serif text in each menu button, just as the Bar Menu does. Child page drop-down menus appear to the right of the Vertical Menu rather than below, as it is with the Horizontal and Bar Menus. You can insert a vertical menu widget by dragging-and-dropping one from the Widgets Library panel onto a master page.

Drag-and-drop the Vertical Menu widget

1. Choose **Plan Mode** from the **View** menu.

    TIMESAVER *Press Cmd+M (Mac) or Ctrl+M (Win) to apply the Plan Mode command quickly.*

2. Double-click a master page thumbnail from the sitemap.

    Muse opens the master page in Design Mode.

3. If it's not visible already, choose **Window > Widgets Library** to display the Widgets Library panel.

4. Click the right-facing arrow next to **Menus** in the **Widgets Library** panel.

    Muse displays the available widget menu options, including **Bar**, **Horizontal**, and **Vertical**.

5. Click and drag the **Vertical** menu from the **Widgets Library** panel onto the header area of the master page.

    IMPORTANT *By default, the Include Page in Navigation option is enabled for each page in the sitemap. As a result, all of the pages in the sitemap automatically appear in the widget menu when you drag it onto the page. Also, any edits you make to the pages in the sitemap (rearranging, renaming, deleting) automatically update in the menu.*

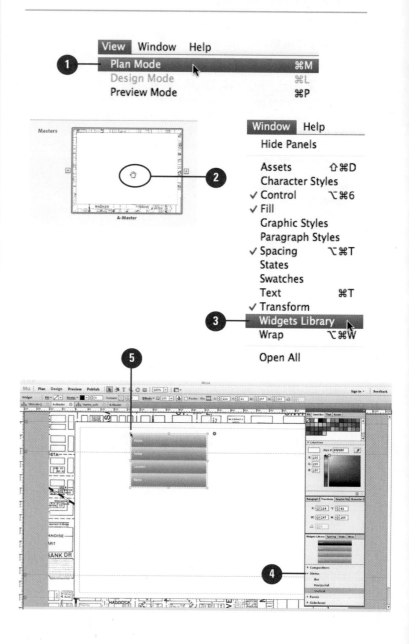

Adding Drop-Down Menus

Any child pages that you add to the sitemap (see Chapter 3, "Creating and Planning a Website"), automatically appear as drop-down menus in the nav bars. However, in order for them to appear, you must first open the nav bar Options window and tell Muse to recognize all pages. The default formatting for drop-down menus is a white fill with black sans-serif text, but keep in mind that you can edit drop-down menus at any time, just as you can nav bars.

Choose the All Pages Menu Type option

① Choose **Plan Mode** from the **View** menu.

TIMESAVER *Press Cmd+M (Mac) or Ctrl+M (Win) to apply the Plan Mode command quickly.*

② From the sitemap, double-click the master page thumbnail for the master you would like to edit.

Muse opens the master page in Design Mode.

③ Click the **Selection Tool** icon at the top of the Design Mode interface.

④ Click the menu to select it.

⑤ Click the right-facing arrow that appears in the upper-right corner of the menu.

Muse displays a flyout options panel.

⑥ In the flyout options panel, choose **All Pages** from the **Menu Type** list.

Muse automatically adds any existing child pages from the sitemap in a new drop-down menu.

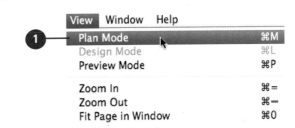

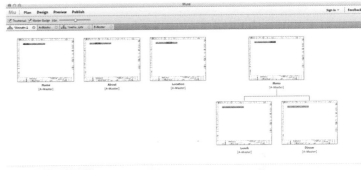

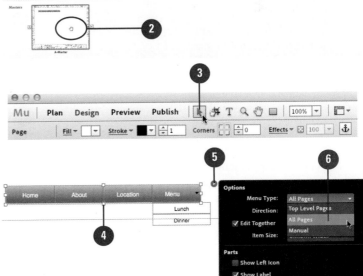

Editing Menu Fill Colors

The fill colors and gradients that appear as part of the default widget formatting are indeed very plain and uninspiring. More likely than not, the default fill colors will not match your site's design. Thankfully, you can easily customize the menus in Design Mode to something that works much better. All you have to do is select one of the rectangles from the menu group and choose a different Fill color from the Fill panel. If you like the linear gradient look, you can change the gradient colors as well. By enabling the Edit Together option, you can apply the same fill color to all of the rectangles in the menu at once.

Use the Edit Together option

1. Choose **Plan Mode** from the **View** menu.

   TIMESAVER *Press Cmd+M (Mac) or Ctrl+M (Win) to apply the Plan Mode command quickly.*

2. From the sitemap, double-click the thumbnail of the page whose menu you'd like to edit.

   Muse opens the page in Design Mode.

3. Click the **Selection Tool** icon at the top of the Design Mode interface.

4. Double-click one of the rectangle frames that make up the menu to select it.

5. Click the **Fill** button in the Control panel to access a drop-down **Fill** panel.

6. In the **Fill Type** section of the **Fill** drop-down panel, choose **Solid** or **Gradient**.

7. Enter a percentage value for the color fill in the **Opacity** field.

   IMPORTANT *By default, the Fill Opacity value is set to 100% (completely opaque). Lowering the Opacity value enables you to see through the fill to the background color underneath.*

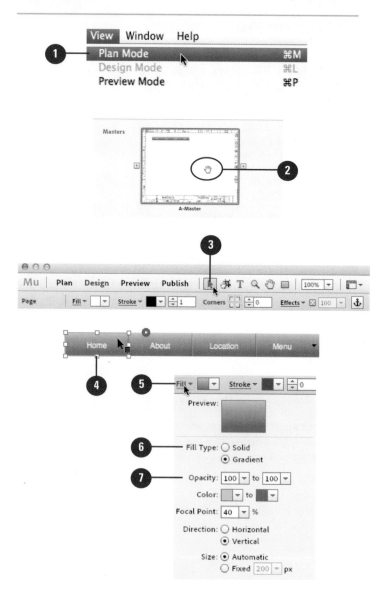

8 Click the **Color** swatch to access a flyout Color Picker.

9 Choose a fill color with the Color Picker via any of the following methods:

◆ Enter values into the **RGB** fields.

◆ Enter a hexadecimal code in the **Hex#** field.

◆ Click a **swatch** from the saved **color swatch list**.

◆ Drag the **Hue** slider up or down to select a color hue. Then click in the color field to the right of the Hue slider to determine the saturation and brightness of the selected color.

◆ Click the **Sample Color** tool icon. To sample a color for the fill, proceed to click anywhere on the page—including in a placed photo or graphic.

Click away to apply the new fill color.

10 Click the right-facing arrow that appears in the upper-right corner of the selected rectangle.

Muse displays a flyout options panel.

11 In the flyout options panel, enable the **Edit Together** option.

IMPORTANT *The Edit Together option is enabled by default.*

Muse automatically applies the new fill attributes to all of the menu buttons.

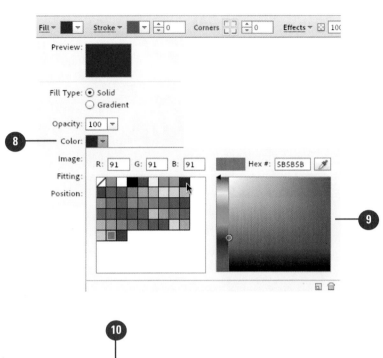

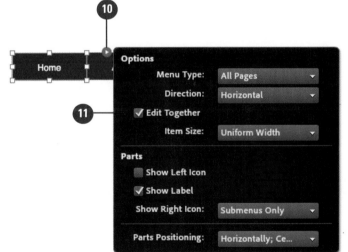

Editing Menu Text Attributes

By default, the widget menu text is set to a cross-platform, sans-serif font recognized by all browsers. You can replace the default font by selecting any one of the menu's text frames and choosing a different font from the Control panel Font list. Note that all of the cross-platform, browser-friendly fonts are located at the top of the Font list. System fonts appear below the dividing line in the Font list and export as images when used in a layout (see Chapter 7, "Working with Text"). You can edit additional menu text formatting, such as font size, text color, and letter spacing, by choosing different options from the Control panel or Text panel.

Use the Edit Together option

1 Choose **Plan Mode** from the **View** menu.

2 From the sitemap, double-click the thumbnail of the page whose menu you'd like to edit.

Muse opens the page in Design Mode.

3 Click the **Selection Tool** icon at the top of the Design Mode interface.

4 Triple-click one of the rectangle frames that make up the menu to select the text frame.

5 Double-click the page name in the selected frame.

Muse switches to the Text tool and displays text attributes in the Control panel.

6 Choose a font for the menu text from the Control panel **Font** list.

7 Enter a size for the menu text in the Control panel **Size** field.

8 To apply a font style, click one of the **Font Style** buttons in the Control panel. Options include **Bold**, **Italic**, and **Underline**.

9 To apply an alignment option, click one of the **Alignment** buttons in the Control panel. Options include **Align Left**, **Align Center**, **Align Right**, and **Align Justify**.

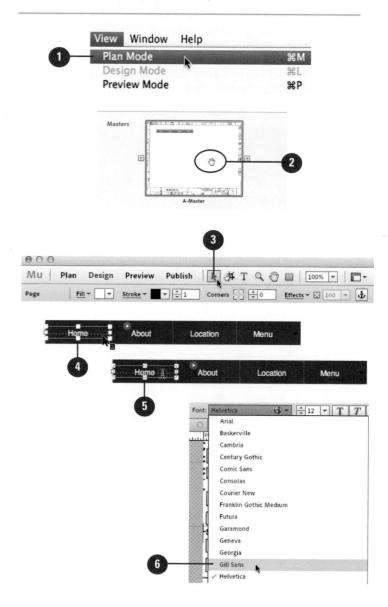

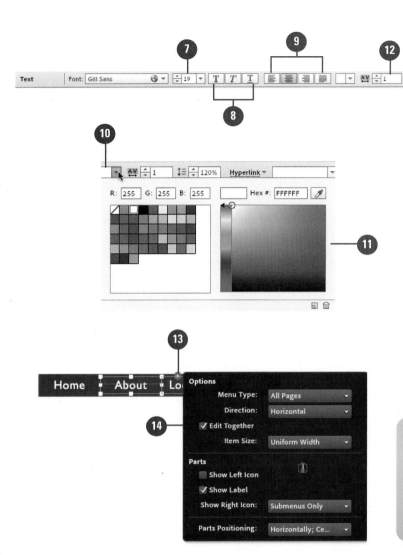

10 From the Control panel, click the **Text Color** button to access the flyout Color Picker.

11 Choose a text color with the Color Picker via any of the following methods:

◆ Enter values into the **RGB** fields.

◆ Enter a hexadecimal code in the **Hex#** field.

◆ Click a **swatch** from the saved **color swatch list**.

◆ Drag the **Hue** slider up or down to select a color hue. Then click in the color field to the right of the Hue slider to determine the saturation and brightness of the selected color.

◆ Click the **Sample Color** tool icon. To sample a color for the text, proceed to click anywhere on the page—including in a placed photo or graphic.

Click away to apply the new text color.

12 Enter a spacing value for the menu text in the Control panel **Letter Space** field.

13 Click the right-facing arrow that appears in the upper-right corner of the selected rectangle.

Muse displays a flyout options panel.

14 In the flyout options panel, enable the **Edit Together** option.

IMPORTANT *The Edit Together option is enabled by default.*

Muse automatically applies the new text attributes to all of the menu buttons.

Editing Menu Size and Spacing

The menu widgets are extremely flexible and can easily be resized to accommodate larger text or rollover images. The Spacing panel enables you to edit the width and height of a menu, as well as the space between menu buttons (referred to as the "gutter"). You can also quickly resize a widget menu by selecting it with the Selection tool and clicking and dragging any side or corner node.

Edit with the Spacing panel

① Choose **Plan Mode** from the **View** menu.

② From the sitemap, double-click the thumbnail of the page whose menu you'd like to edit.

Muse opens the page in Design Mode.

③ Click the **Selection Tool** icon at the top of the Design Mode interface.

④ Click the menu to select it.

⑤ Choose **Window > Spacing** to display the **Spacing** panel.

⑥ In the **Spacing** panel, change the height of the menu by increasing the **Top** and **Bottom Padding** settings.

⑦ Change the width of the menu by increasing the **Left** and **Right Padding** settings.

⑧ Change the spacing between pages in the menu by increasing the **Horizontal** and **Vertical Gutter** settings.

Did You Know?

You can also resize a menu using the Selection tool. To do so, click the menu to select it, and then click and drag any side or corner node. Hold down Shift as you drag to constrain overall proportions as you resize the menu.

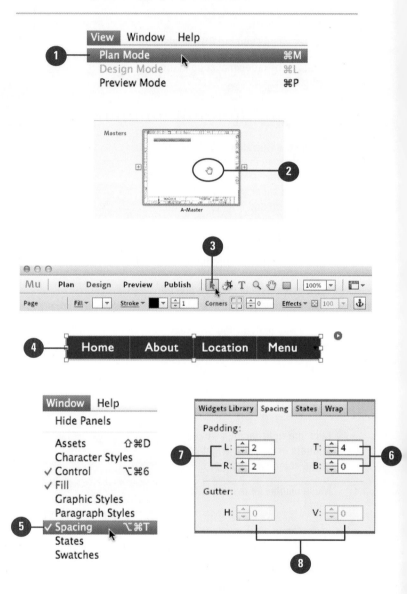

Editing Menu Rollover States

The States panel enables you to edit the appearance of your menu button states. The Normal state represents the button's default appearance. Rollover is how the button appears when the mouse is rolling over it. Mouse Down represents the clicked-on state of the button, and the Active state represents the menu button's appearance when you are actually viewing that page in a browser. You can edit each of these states by selecting one from the States panel and choosing different attributes, such as fill or text color, from the Control panel.

Edit with the States panel

1 Choose **Plan Mode** from the **View** menu.

2 From the sitemap, double-click the thumbnail of the page whose menu you'd like to edit.

Muse opens the page in Design Mode.

3 Click the **Selection Tool** icon at the top of the Design Mode interface.

4 Double-click one of the rectangle frames that make up the menu to select it.

5 Choose **Window > States** to display the **States** panel.

6 Click the **Rollover** state in the States panel.

7 From the **Control** panel, choose the preferred rollover state fill and text attributes (see Editing Menu Fill Colors and Editing Menu Text Attributes in this chapter).

8 Click the **Mouse Down** state in the States panel and repeat Step 7.

9 Click the **Active** state in the States panel and repeat Step 7.

Muse updates the different menu button states. Be sure to click Preview and test them.

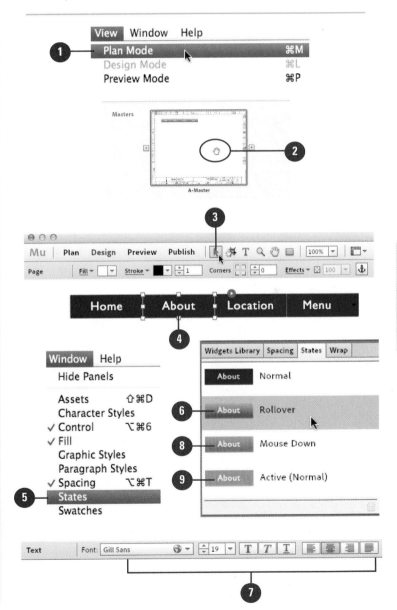

Inserting Active Rollover State Images

The Active rollover state is what the menu button looks like when you are actually viewing the page in a browser. From the States panel, you can choose to place a background image behind the button text whenever the page is being viewed. It's always best to size the image accordingly in an image-editing application, such as Photoshop or Fireworks, but you can also fit or fill the frame when placing it in Muse.

Edit with the States panel

1. Choose **Plan Mode** from the **View** menu.

2. From the sitemap, double-click the thumbnail of the page whose menu you'd like to edit.

   Muse opens the page in Design Mode.

3. Click the **Selection Tool** icon at the top of the Design Mode interface.

4. Double-click one of the rectangle frames that make up the menu to select it.

5. Choose **Window > States** to display the **States** panel.

6. Click the **Active** state in the States panel.

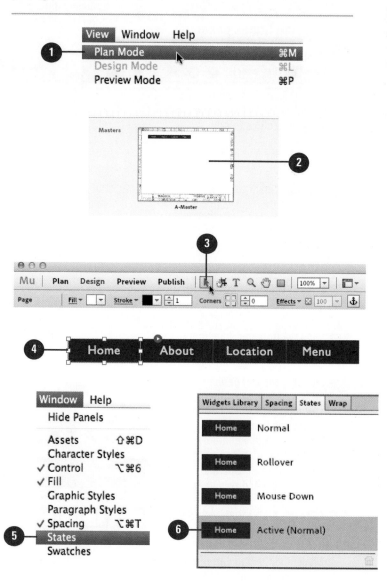

7. Click the **Fill** button in the Control panel to access a drop-down Fill panel.

8. From the drop-down Fill panel, click the **Choose Background Image** button (the folder icon) to acces the Import dialog box.

9. Using the Import dialog box, navigate to the background image on your system disk. Click the image file to select it and then click **Select**.

> **IMPORTANT** *You can only import images saved in the following file formats: PNG, PSD, JPEG, and GIF.*

When Active (viewing the page in a browser), Muse places the chosen image behind the menu button text.

10. Choose a fitting option from the **Fitting** drop-down list. Options include: **Original Size, Scale to Fill, Scale to Fit, Tile, Tile Horizontally,** and **Tile Vertically**.

> **IMPORTANT** *The Tile options enable you to repeat the image in the rectangle. The Tile option repeats the image both horizontally and vertically.*

11. Click one of the small squares next to the **Position** option in the Fill drop-down panel. By doing so, you can determine how the image is positioned in the rectangle relative to which small square you clicked.

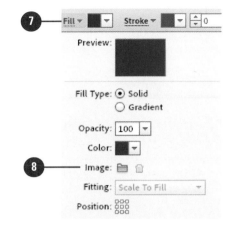

Working with Graphics

5

Introduction

Without photos and graphics, your websites would be pretty boring, now wouldn't they? Without a doubt, graphics play an important role in any layout for any type of media. Web design is no exception.

Thankfully, placing graphics in Muse is incredibly easy. In fact, the entire process is very similar to working in InDesign. Muse contains an Assets panel, which behaves similarly to the Links panel in InDesign. Other shared features include an Edit Original command, a Content Grabber, and the ability to place layered PSD files.

In this chapter, you'll learn the different file types you can import and how to place them onto a page. You'll also learn how to resize graphic frames and their contents, both separately and together.

This chapter also explains how to replace and delete graphics in an existing frame using the Fill panel Image options, and shows you the various ways you can rotate and duplicate objects.

The final sections of the chapter explain how easy it is to give your graphics browser control. You'll learn how to pin a graphic to a specific browser location and set page objects to display at 100% browser width.

Placing a Graphic

The easiest way to place a graphic into your layout is to apply the Place command. Muse enables you to place graphics that have been saved in the following file formats: PNG, PSD, JPEG, and GIF. The GIF format is best used for small, non-transparent web graphics such as logos, icons, and buttons. PNG is a nice alternative to GIF, as it is the native format for Adobe Fireworks and handles transparency better; however, PNG files are usually a little bit larger in file size. The JPEG format is best used for photos, while layered PSD files are best for creating buttons that can be edited directly in Muse (see "Placing a Photoshop [PSD] Button" later in this chapter).

Choose the Place command

1 Choose **Plan Mode** from the **View** menu.

> **TIMESAVER** *Press Cmd+M (Mac) or Ctrl+M (Win) to apply the Plan Mode command quickly.*

2 Double-click any page or master page thumbnail from the sitemap.

Muse opens the page in Design Mode.

3 Choose **File > Place** to access the Import dialog box.

4 Using the Import dialog box, navigate to the background image on your system disk. Click the image file to select it and then click **Select**.

> **IMPORTANT** *You can only import images saved in the following file formats: PNG, PSD, JPEG, and GIF.*

5 Click the loaded place cursor anywhere on the page to place the image at its actual size (100%).

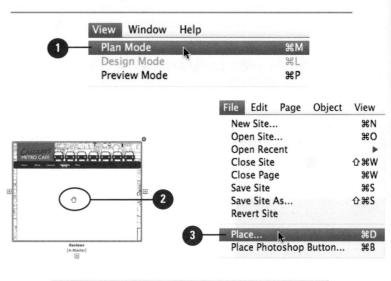

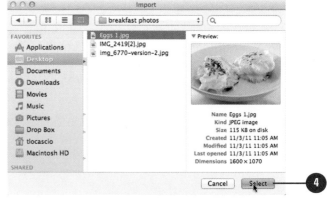

Importing a Graphic by Dragging-and-Dropping

Another way to import graphics is to drag-and-drop them into a Muse layout from the Finder (Mac OSX) or Explorer (Windows). All you need to do is navigate to the PNG, PSD, JPEG, or GIF file on your system disk; then select it, and drag it into your Muse layout. As soon as you move the cursor over the layout, Muse displays the loaded place cursor, which features a thumbnail of the graphic next to the selection arrow. Click anywhere on the page to place it at its actual size (100%).

Drag from the Finder (Mac OSX) or Explorer (Windows)

1. Choose **Plan Mode** from the **View** menu.

   TIMESAVER *Press Cmd+M (Mac) or Ctrl+M (Win) to apply the Plan Mode command quickly.*

2. Double-click any page or master page thumbnail from the sitemap.

   Muse opens the page in Design Mode.

3. Select the image in Finder (Mac OSX) or Explorer (Windows).

4. Drag-and-drop the selected image onto the Muse page.

5. Click the loaded place cursor anywhere on the page to place the image at its actual size (100%).

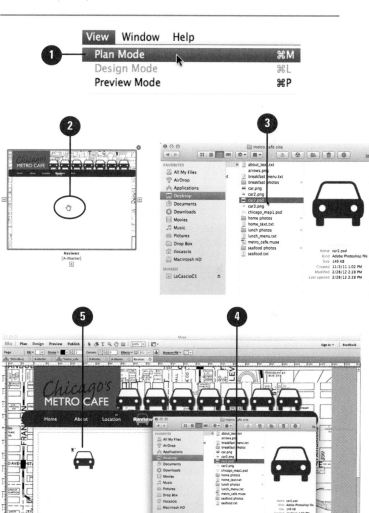

Resizing a Graphic

Drag a side or corner node with the Selection tool

1 Choose **Plan Mode** from the **View** menu.

> **TIMESAVER** *Press Cmd+M (Mac) or Ctrl+M (Win) to apply the Plan Mode command quickly.*

2 From the sitemap, double-click the thumbnail of the page whose graphic you'd like to resize.

Muse opens the page in Design Mode.

3 Click the **Selection Tool** icon at the top of the Design Mode interface.

4 Click the graphic to select it.

5 Click and drag any corner or side node to resize the selected graphic.

> **IMPORTANT** *As you resize the graphic, Muse displays the current scale percentage next to the Selection tool cursor.*

Did You Know?

You can also resize a graphic without resizing its frame container. To do so, double-click the graphic with the Selection tool to select the contents. Muse displays the image boundaries. Click and drag any boundary node to resize the contents without also resizing the container.

The best way to size your web graphics is to do so using an image editing application, such as Adobe Fireworks or Adobe Photoshop. However, as you're creating your initial layouts in Muse, you may not know exactly what pixel dimensions you want to use for each graphic. In this instance, you can resize graphics on the fly, directly in Muse. Keep in mind that you should never scale a graphic higher than its actual size (100%), or you risk losing overall image quality, thereby causing the image to display poorly.

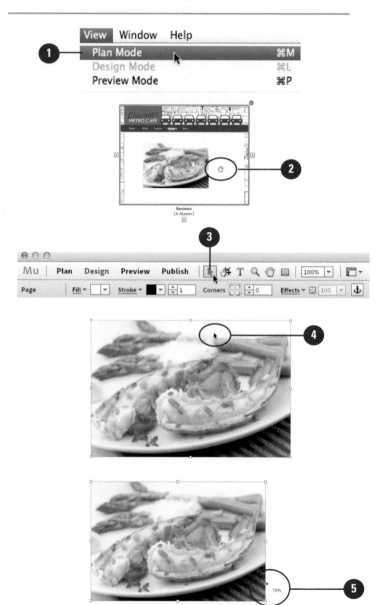

Cropping a Graphic

Drag a side or corner node with the Crop tool

1 Choose **Plan Mode** from the **View** menu.

TIMESAVER *Press Cmd+M (Mac) or Ctrl+M (Win) to apply the Plan Mode command quickly.*

2 From the sitemap, double-click the thumbnail of the page whose graphic you'd like to resize.

Muse opens the page in Design Mode.

3 Click the **Crop Tool** icon at the top of the Design Mode interface.

4 Click the graphic to select it.

5 Click and drag any corner or side node to resize the graphic frame.

Some web graphics, such as photographs, may contain more imagery than you need to display in a certain layout. With Muse, you can adjust the crop of an image by changing the size of its frame container. The Crop tool enables you to drag any side or corner selection node and resize a frame, without resizing its graphic contents. You can also change the size of a graphic frame numerically, by entering new width and height values in the Control panel or Transform panel.

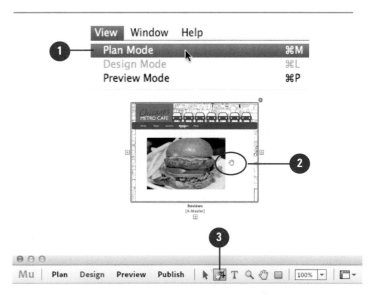

Change the Width and Height settings

1. Choose **Plan Mode** from the **View** menu.

   TIMESAVER *Press Cmd+M (Mac) or Ctrl+M (Win) to apply the Plan Mode command quickly.*

2. From the sitemap, double-click the thumbnail of the page whose graphic you'd like to resize.

   Muse opens the page in Design Mode.

3. Click the **Selection Tool** icon at the top of the Design Mode interface.

4. Click the graphic to select it.

5. Enter new pixel values in the **Control** panel **Width** and **Height** fields.

   Muse resizes the selected graphic frame.

Did You Know?

You can also enter Width and Height values in the Transform panel. To display the Transform panel, choose Transform from the Window menu.

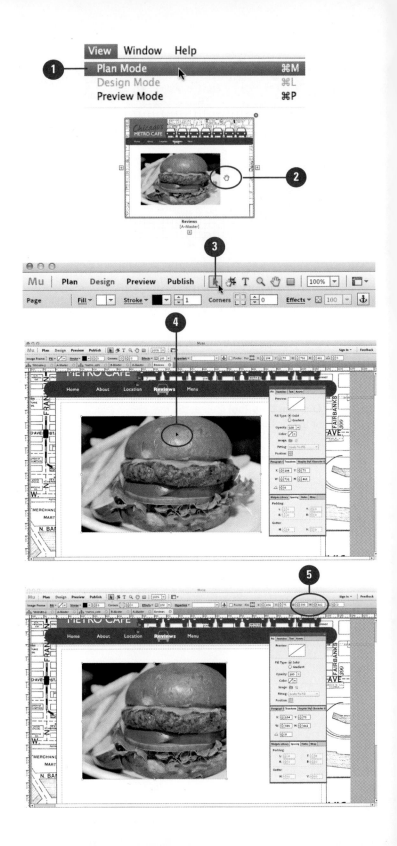

Repositioning a Graphic Inside a Frame

Another way you can change the crop of an image is to reposition it inside of its frame container. When you select the Crop tool and hover the cursor over a placed image, Muse displays a circle icon—called the Content Grabber—in the center of the frame. By dragging the Content Grabber, you can reposition the image inside the frame. You can also reposition a graphic inside of a frame by double-clicking it with the Selection tool and dragging.

Click and drag the Content Grabber

1 Choose **Plan Mode** from the **View** menu.

TIMESAVER *Press Cmd+M (Mac) or Ctrl+M (Win) to apply the Plan Mode command quickly.*

2 From the sitemap, double-click the thumbnail of the page whose graphic you'd like to resize.

Muse opens the page in Design Mode.

3 Click the **Crop Tool** icon at the top of the Design Mode interface.

4 Hover the cursor over the center of the placed graphic until the **Content Grabber** (the circle icon) appears.

5 Click and drag the **Content Grabber** to reposition the graphic inside the frame.

Did You Know?

You can also use the Selection tool to reposition a graphic inside of a frame. To do so, double-click the graphic with the Selection tool to select the contents. Muse displays the image boundaries. Click and drag the image to reposition it inside the container.

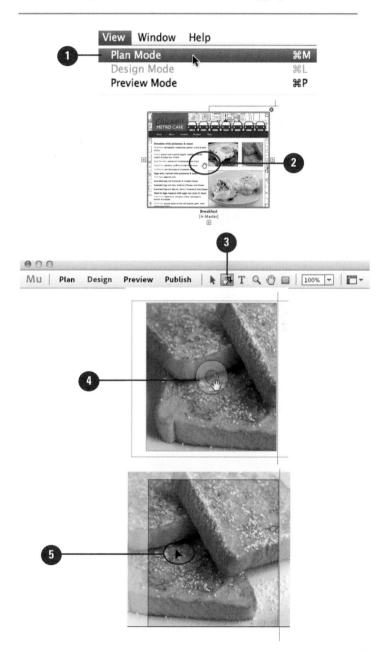

Filling a Frame with an Image

Another way to place graphics in Muse is to select an existing frame and click the Image Import button, which is located in the Fill panel. When you apply this method, Muse enables you to choose how you'd like to fit the image inside the frame. The Fill panel Scale to Fill option enables you to automatically resize the image proportionally to fill the frame. Just be sure not to scale the image above its actual size (100%), or you could compromise the image's quality (see "Resizing a Graphic" earlier in this chapter).

Place graphics using the Fill panel Image option

1. Choose **Plan Mode** from the **View** menu.

   TIMESAVER *Press Cmd+M (Mac) or Ctrl+M (Win) to apply the Plan Mode command quickly.*

2. Double-click any page or master page thumbnail from the sitemap.

   Muse opens the page in Design Mode.

3. Click the **Rectangle Tool** icon at the top of the Design Mode interface.

   TIMESAVER *Press M to access the Rectangle tool quickly.*

4. Click and drag anywhere on the page to draw a rectangle with the **Rectangle tool**.

5. Click the **Fill** button in the Control panel to access a drop-down Fill panel.

6. From the drop-down Fill panel, click the **Image** button (the folder icon) to access the Import dialog box.

Did You Know?

You can also access Fitting settings in the Fill panel. To display the Fill panel, choose Fill from the Window menu.

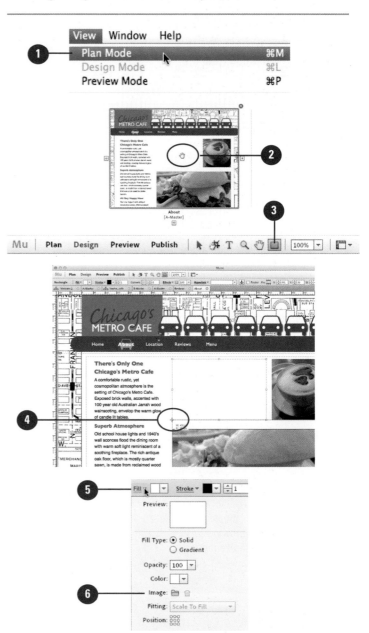

7 Using the Import dialog box, navigate to the image on your system disk. Click the image file to select it and then click **Select**.

IMPORTANT *You can only import images saved in the following file formats: PNG, PSD, JPEG, and GIF.*

8 Choose **Scale to Fill** from the **Fitting** drop-down list.

9 Click the small center square next to the **Position** option in the Fill drop-down panel. By doing so, you can center the image in the rectangle.

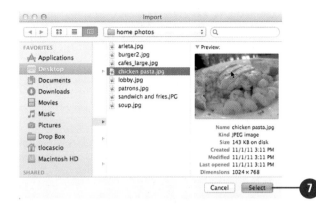

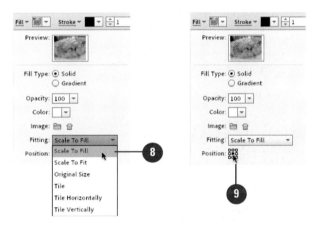

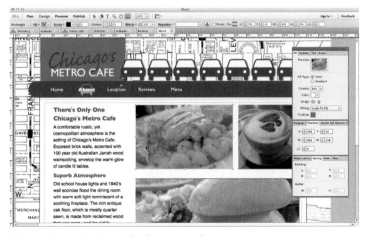

Muse places the image in the rectangle.

Replacing a Graphic

If you already have an image placed in a frame, but later decide to swap it out with another, you can do so by selecting the frame and clicking the Fill panel Image button. Doing so enables you to select another graphic from your hard disk and replace the current one. The Fill panel also enables you to choose Fitting and Position options for the replacement graphic.

Replace graphics using the Fill panel Image option

1. Choose **Plan Mode** from the **View** menu.

   TIMESAVER *Press Cmd+M (Mac) or Ctrl+M (Win) to apply the Plan Mode command quickly.*

2. From the sitemap, double-click the thumbnail of the page whose graphic you'd like to replace.

   Muse opens the page in Design Mode.

3. Click the **Selection Tool** icon at the top of the Design Mode interface.

   TIMESAVER *Press V to access the Selection tool quickly.*

4. Click the graphic to select it.

5. Click the **Fill** button in the Control panel to access a drop-down Fill panel.

6. From the drop-down Fill panel, click the **Image** button (the folder icon) to access the Import dialog box.

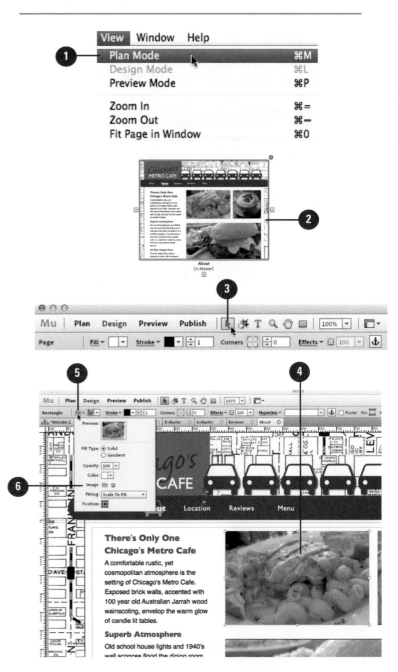

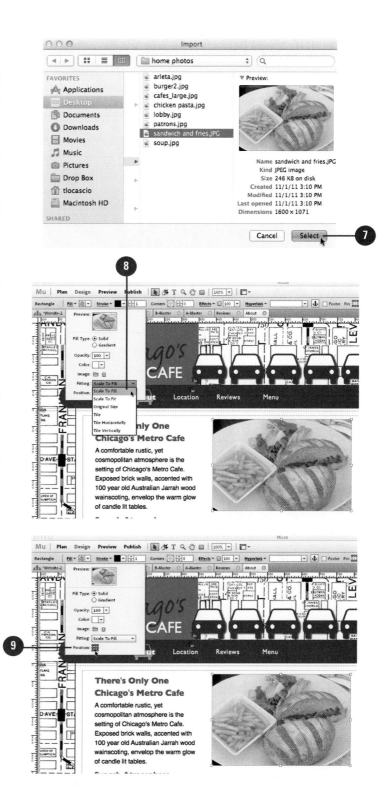

⑦ Using the Import dialog box, navigate to the image on your system disk. Click the image file to select it and then click **Select**.

IMPORTANT *You can only import images saved in the following file formats: PNG, PSD, JPEG, and GIF.*

⑧ Choose a fitting option from the **Fitting** drop-down list. Options include: **Original Size, Scale to Fill, Scale to Fit, Tile, Tile Horizontally,** and **Tile Vertically**.

IMPORTANT *The Tile options enable you to repeat the image in the rectangle. The Tile option repeats the image both horizontally and vertically.*

⑨ Click one of the small squares next to the **Position** option in the Fill drop-down panel. By doing so, you can determine how the image is positioned in the rectangle relative to where you clicked.

Deleting a Graphic

By using the Fill panel Image options, you can delete a placed graphic and retain its frame container. You can do so by selecting the graphic and clicking the Clear Background Image button (the Trash Can icon) in the Fill panel. This enables you to keep the frame in the layout as a placeholder and import a different graphic into it at a later time.

Remove a graphic using the Fill panel Image option

1 Choose **Plan Mode** from the **View** menu.

> **TIMESAVER** *Press Cmd+M (Mac) or Ctrl+M (Win) to apply the Plan Mode command quickly.*

2 From the sitemap, double-click the thumbnail of the page whose graphic you'd like to resize.

Muse opens the page in Design Mode.

3 Click the **Selection Tool** icon at the top of the Design Mode interface.

> **TIMESAVER** *Press V to access the Selection tool quickly.*

4 Click the graphic to select it.

5 Click the **Fill** button in the Control panel to access a drop-down Fill panel.

6 From the drop-down Fill panel, click the **Clear Background Image** button (the Trash Can icon) to delete the placed graphic.

Muse deletes the graphic contents while maintaining the graphic frame.

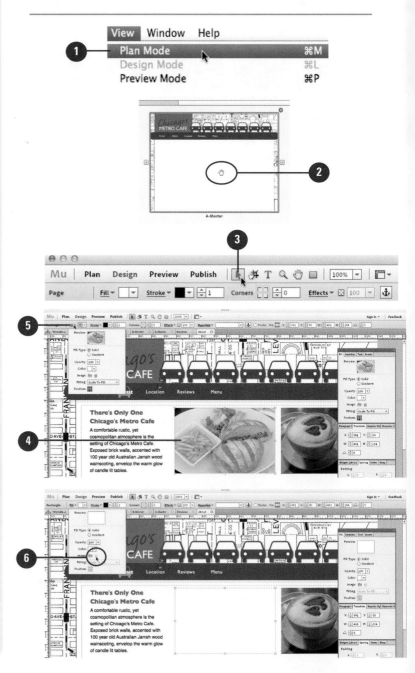

Rotating an Object

Rotating objects in Muse is really no different from rotating objects in Adobe InDesign or Illustrator. You can rotate selected objects on the fly by dragging a corner node with the Selection tool, or to a specific angle by entering a value in the Rotation Angle field of the Control panel or Transform panel. When entering values in the Rotation Angle field, you must remember to enter positive values to rotate clockwise and negative values to rotate counterclockwise.

Rotate with the Selection tool

1. Choose **Plan Mode** from the **View** menu.

   TIMESAVER *Press Cmd+M (Mac) or Ctrl+M (Win) to apply the Plan Mode command quickly.*

2. From the sitemap, double-click the thumbnail of the page whose object you'd like to rotate.

   Muse opens the page in Design Mode.

3. Click the **Selection Tool** icon at the top of the Design Mode interface.

   TIMESAVER *Press V to access the Selection tool quickly.*

4. Click the object to select it.

5. Hover the cursor next to any corner selection node.

   Muse displays the rotate cursor.

6. Click and drag down to rotate clockwise; click and drag up to rotate counterclockwise.

Did You Know?

You can also rotate an image without also roatating its frame container. To do so, double-click the image with the Selection tool and hover the cursor over any corner node. Drag to rotate the image within its stationary frame container.

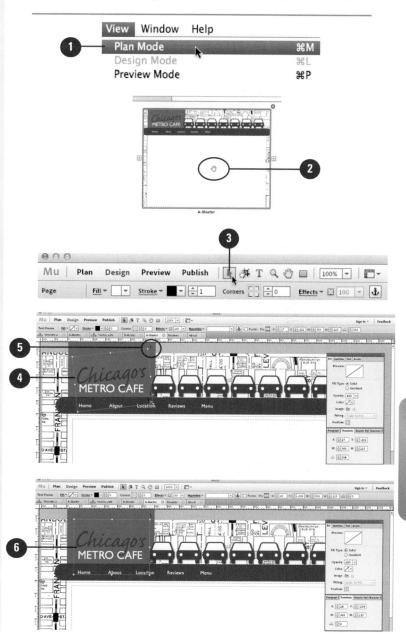

Enter a value in the Rotation Angle field

① Choose **Plan Mode** from the **View** menu.

TIMESAVER *Press Cmd+M (Mac) or Ctrl+M (Win) to apply the Plan Mode command quickly.*

② From the sitemap, double-click the thumbnail of the page whose graphic you'd like to rotate.

Muse opens the page in Design Mode.

③ Click the **Selection Tool** icon at the top of the Design Mode interface.

TIMESAVER *Press V to access the Selection tool quickly.*

④ Click the graphic to select it.

⑤ In the Control panel, enter a value in the **Rotation Angle** field.

IMPORTANT *Enter positive numbers to rotate clockwise; enter negative numbers to rotate counterclockwise.*

Muse applies the rotation angle to the selected graphic.

Did You Know?

You can also enter Rotation Angle values in the Transform panel. To display the Transform panel, choose Transform from the Window menu.

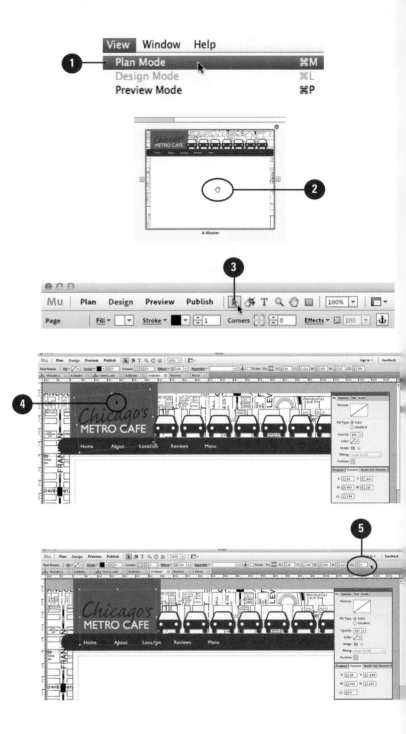

Duplicating an Object

The best way to handle repeating graphics is to tile them in a single graphic frame using the Fill panel Fitting options. Doing so keeps the overall file size of your pages small, so that the viewer does not have to wait a long time for them to load in a browser. However, should your design include duplicate graphics that cannot be tiled due to their nonconsecutive placement on the page, you can duplicate selected graphics easily by applying the Duplicate command or by Option-(Mac) or Alt-(Win) dragging them.

Choose the Duplicate command

1 Choose **Plan Mode** from the **View** menu.

> **TIMESAVER** *Press Cmd+M (Mac) or Ctrl+M (Win) to apply the Plan Mode command quickly.*

2 From the sitemap, double-click the thumbnail of the page whose object you'd like to duplicate.

> Muse opens the page in Design Mode.

3 Click the **Selection Tool** icon at the top of the Design Mode interface.

> **TIMESAVER** *Press V to access the Selection tool quickly.*

4 Click the graphic to select it.

5 Choose **Duplicate** from the **Edit** menu.

> **TIMESAVER** *Press Shift+Cmd+D (Mac) or Shift+Ctrl+D (Win) to apply the Duplicate command quickly.*

Muse creates a duplicate of the selected object and places it adjacent to the original. The duplicate object remains selected while the original does not.

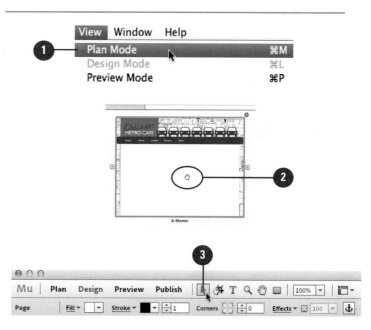

Muse duplicates the object.

Option/Alt-drag the graphic

1 Choose **Plan Mode** from the **View** menu.

> **TIMESAVER** *Press Cmd+M (Mac) or Ctrl+M (Win) to apply the Plan Mode command quickly.*

2 From the sitemap, double-click the thumbnail of the page whose graphic you'd like to duplicate.

Muse opens the page in Design Mode.

3 Click the **Selection Tool** icon at the top of the Design Mode interface.

> **TIMESAVER** *Press V to access the Selection tool quickly.*

4 Click the graphic to select it.

5 To create a duplicate, hold down Option (Mac) or Alt (Win) and drag in any direction.

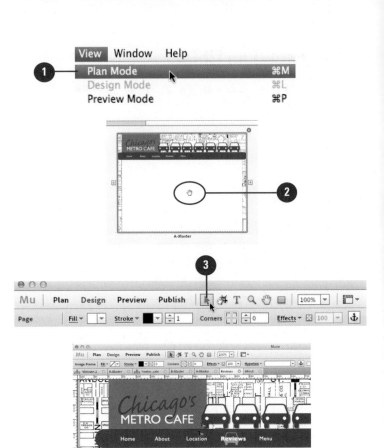

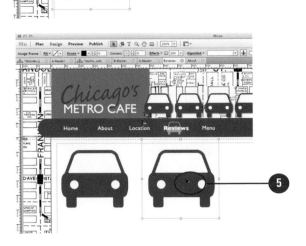

Placing a Photoshop (PSD) Button

One of the great things about working with Muse is that you can place native Photoshop files. By placing graphics saved in the PSD format, you can access the different layers contained in the file and apply them to specific button rollover states in Muse. You can do so directly from the Photoshop Import Options dialog box. Creating dynamic web buttons has never been so easy!

Choose the Place Photoshop Button command

1 Choose **Plan Mode** from the **View** menu.

TIMESAVER *Press Cmd+M (Mac) or Ctrl+M (Win) to apply the Plan Mode command quickly.*

2 Double-click any page or master page thumbnail from the sitemap.

Muse opens the page in Design Mode.

3 Choose **File > Place Photoshop Button** to access the Place Photoshop Button dialog box.

TIMESAVER *Press Cmd+B (Mac) or Ctrl+B (Win) to apply the Place Photoshop Button command quickly.*

4 Using the Place Photoshop Button dialog box, navigate to the PSD image on your system disk. Click the image file to select it and then click **Select**.

Muse displays the Photoshop Import Options dialog box.

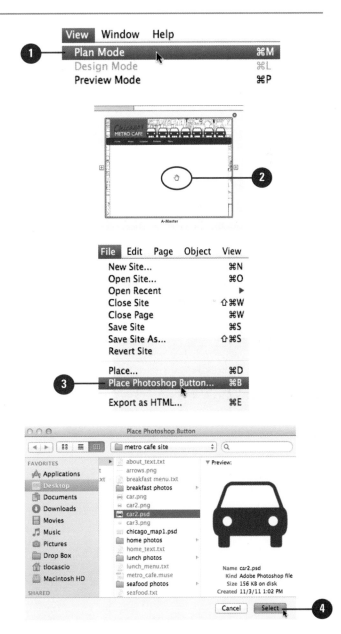

5. Using the Photoshop Import Options dialog box, choose a Photoshop layer to apply as the **Normal State**.

6. Choose a Photoshop layer to apply as the **Rollover State**.

7. Choose a Photoshop layer to apply as the **Mouse Down State**.

8. Choose a Photoshop layer to apply as the **Active State**.

9. Click OK to close the Photoshop Import Options dialog box and apply the import options.

10. Click the loaded place cursor anywhere on the page to place the image at its actual size (100%).

11. To test the button, choose **Preview** from the **View** menu or click the **Preview** button above the Control panel.

See Also

See Chapter 4, "Adding Navigational Content," to learn more about working with rollover states in a menu.

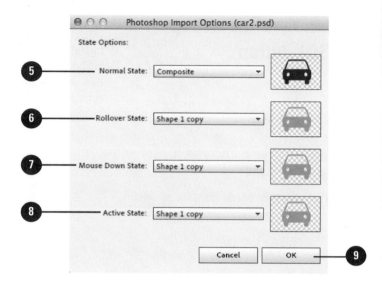

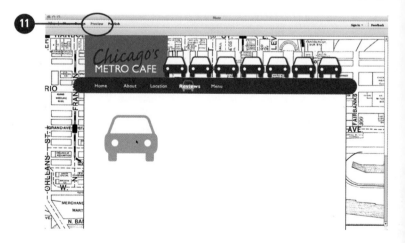

Using Edit Original

Although it is treated as a separate Adobe product, Muse is truly integrated with the Creative Suite. Not only can you place native Photoshop files (see "Placing a Photoshop [PSD] Button" earlier in this chapter), but you can also utilize round-trip editing of all your placed graphics. By selecting the graphic from the Assets panel and choosing Edit Original from the contextual menu, you can open the graphic in its native application, such as Photoshop, Fireworks, or Illustrator, and apply edits to it. When you return to Muse, the graphic automatically updates.

Choose the Edit Original command

1. Choose **Plan Mode** from the **View** menu.

   TIMESAVER *Press Cmd+M (Mac) or Ctrl+M (Win) to apply the Plan Mode command quickly.*

2. From the sitemap, double-click the thumbnail of the page whose graphic you'd like to edit.

   Muse opens the page in Design Mode.

3. Click the **Selection Tool** icon at the top of the Design Mode interface.

   TIMESAVER *Press V to access the Selection tool quickly.*

4. Click the graphic to select it.

5. Display the Assets panel by choosing **Window > Assets**.

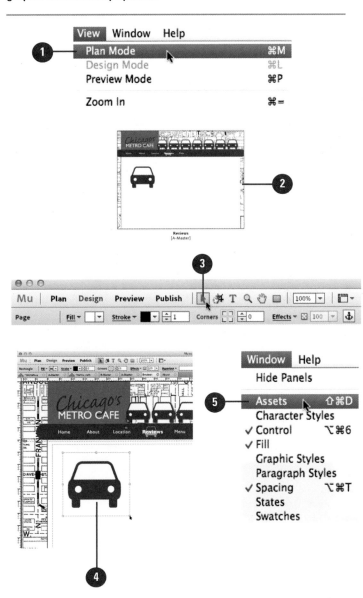

Working with Graphics **83**

6 Locate the name of the graphic from the Assets panel list. Right-click or Control-click (Mac) the name to access the contextual menu and choose **Edit Original**.

Muse opens the graphic in its native application.

7 Proceed to edit the graphic in its native application and then choose **File > Save**.

Muse automatically updates the placed graphic.

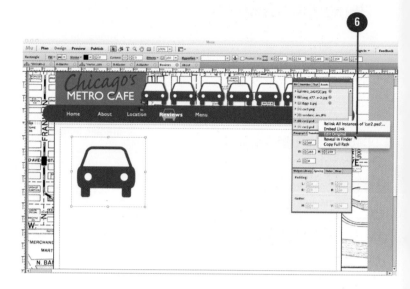

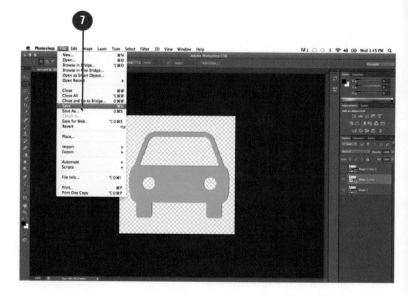

Pinning a Graphic

Another unique feature in Muse is the ability to pin a graphic to a specific browser location. By selecting a graphic and choosing a Pin position from the Control panel, you can force the graphic to stay in position as the viewer scrolls through the page in a browser. It's that simple!

Pin a graphic to a specific browser location

1 Choose **Plan Mode** from the **View** menu.

> **TIMESAVER** *Press Cmd+M (Mac) or Ctrl+M (Win) to apply the Plan Mode command quickly.*

2 From the sitemap, double-click the thumbnail of the page whose graphic you'd like to edit.

Muse opens the page in Design Mode.

3 Click the **Selection Tool** icon at the top of the Design Mode interface.

> **TIMESAVER** *Press V to access the Selection tool quickly.*

4 Click the graphic to select it.

5 In the Control panel, click a **Pin** position. Doing so pins the graphic to the browser relative to were you clicked. For example, clicking the upper-left square pins the graphic to the upper-left corner of the browser window.

Muse pins the graphic to the chosen browser location.

6 To view the pinned graphic, choose **Preview** from the **View** menu or click the **Preview** button above the Control panel.

The pinned graphic stays in position as you scroll the page.

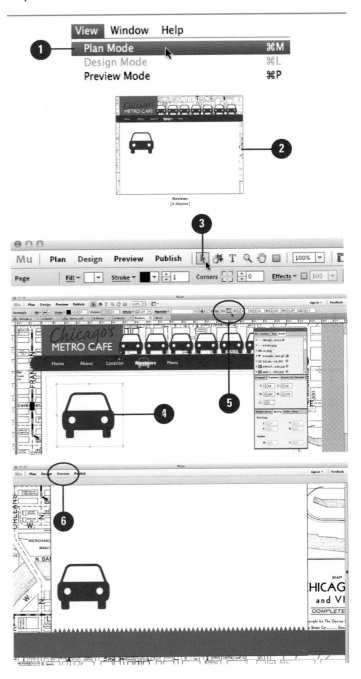

Setting Objects to Display at 100% Browser Width

Another useful feature in Muse is the ability to set objects to display at 100% browser width. This is especially useful when setting up objects on master pages, because it enables the objects to resize with the browser window—an effect you would usually want to keep consistent throughout your site pages. These objects can contain color fills or tiled background images.

Create rectangles that resize with the Browser window

1 Choose **Plan Mode** from the **View** menu.

> **TIMESAVER** *Press Cmd+M (Mac) or Ctrl+M (Win) to apply the Plan Mode command quickly.*

2 From the sitemap, double-click the thumbnail of the page that you'd like to add a graphic to at 100% browser width.

Muse opens the page in Design Mode.

3 Click the **Rectangle Tool** icon at the top of the Design Mode interface.

> **TIMESAVER** *Press M to access the Rectangle tool quickly.*

4 Click and drag with the Rectangle tool to create the shape. Proceed to apply the desired fill and stroke attributes.

> **IMPORTANT** *As you draw with the Rectangle tool, Muse displays the current width and height measurements (in pixels) next to the cursor.*

5 Hold down Cmd (Mac) or Ctrl (Win) to temporarily access the Selection tool. Click and drag the left and right side nodes to align them with the edges of the page. Release the mouse button when the red highlight appears.

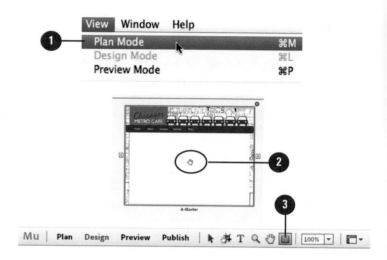

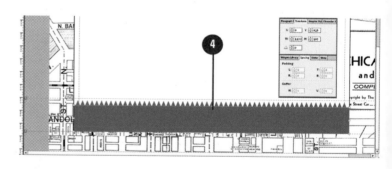

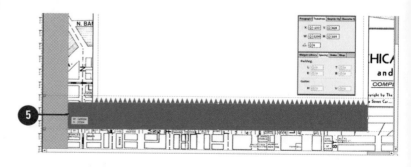

Working with Graphic Styles and Effects

6

Introduction

One of the great things about working with Muse is that it gives you the ability to apply graphic effects, such as drop shadows, bevels, and glows. There is no need to apply these effects in a separate application, such as Photoshop, Fireworks, or Illustrator.

In this chapter, you'll learn how to enable these effects in the Effects panel. You'll also learn how to choose effect options, such as drop shadow color, bevel size, glow opacity, and more.

In addition, this chapter shows you how to create text wraps by placing graphics as an inline objects in a text frame. It also explains how to apply rounded edges to all four corners of a rectangle at once, as well as to the individual corners.

In the final sections of this chapter, you'll learn how to save your favorites combinations of object style attributes—such as fill color, wrap spacing, and effects—as a graphic style. By doing so, you can apply these attributes to other objects in your websites with the single click of a mouse button.

Creating a Text Wrap

A text wrap enables you to place a graphic next to a body of text and force the lines of text to wrap around the shape of the graphic. To create this effect in Muse, you must first select the graphic and cut it to the Clipboard. You can then use the Text tool to place the graphic as an inline object in the text frame. After you place the graphic in the body of text, you can choose the preferred position and offset options from the Wrap panel.

Choose wrap options for placed inline graphics

1. Choose **Plan Mode** from the **View** menu.

   TIMESAVER *Press Cmd+M (Mac) or Ctrl+M (Win) to apply the Plan Mode command quickly.*

2. From the sitemap, double-click the thumbnail of the page on which you'd like to create a text wrap.

   Muse opens the page in Design Mode.

3. Click the **Selection Tool** icon at the top of the Design Mode interface.

   TIMESAVER *Press V to access the Selection tool quickly.*

4. To select the graphic you'd like to add a text wrap to, click it with the Selection tool.

5. Choose **Edit > Cut** to copy the graphic to the Clipboard and remove it from the page.

   TIMESAVER *Press Cmd+X (Mac) or Ctrl+X (Win) to apply the Cut command quickly.*

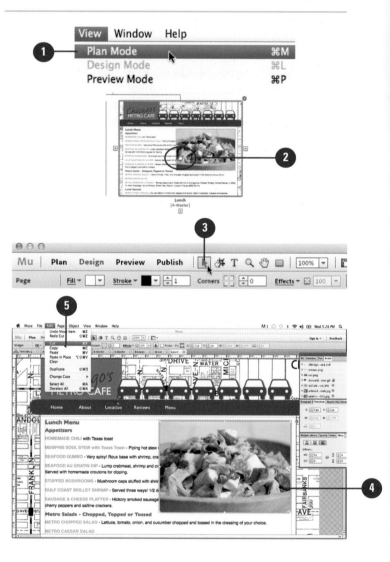

6 Click the **Text Tool** icon at the top of the Design Mode interface.

TIMESAVER *Press T to access the Text tool quickly.*

7 To define an insertion point for the graphic, place the Text tool cursor in a text frame.

8 Choose **Edit > Paste** to insert the graphic as an inline object in the paragraph.

TIMESAVER *Press Cmd+V (Mac) or Ctrl+V (Win) to apply the Paste command quickly.*

9 Choose **Window > Wrap** to display the Wrap panel.

TIMESAVER *Press Option+Cmd+W (Mac) or Alt+Ctrl+W (Win) to display the Wrap panel quickly.*

10 Choose an inline position for the graphic by clicking one of the **Position** buttons located at the top of the Wrap panel. Options include: **Position Object In-Line with Text**, **Position Object to the Left of Text**, **Position Object to the Right of Text**.

11 To apply padding around the inline graphic, enter numeric values in the **Offset** fields of the Wrap panel (top, bottom, left, right).

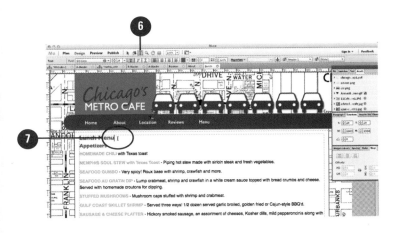

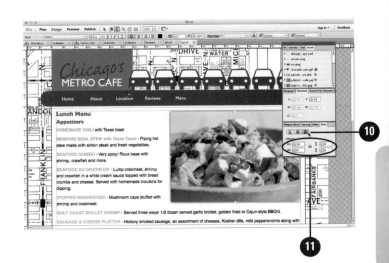

Applying Corner Effects

Another popular design effect you can apply in Muse is corner effects. With corner effects, you can apply rounded corners to rectangular frames. By selecting a frame and entering a radius value in the Control panel Corners field, you can round all four corners of the frame at once. To round a single corner, click the corresponding Corners button in the Control panel and enter a radius value in the neighboring field.

Enable the corner radius buttons

1 Choose **Plan Mode** from the **View** menu.

> **TIMESAVER** *Press Cmd+M (Mac) or Ctrl+M (Win) to apply the Plan Mode command quickly.*

2 From the sitemap, double-click the thumbnail of the page whose frame you'd like to edit.

Muse opens the page in Design Mode.

3 Click the **Selection Tool** icon at the top of the Design Mode interface.

> **TIMESAVER** *Press V to access the Selection tool quickly.*

4 To select the frame you'd like to apply corner effects to, click it with the **Selection** tool.

5 To apply the same corner radius to all four corners, enter a value in the Control panel **Corners** field.

6 To apply a corner radius to a specific corner, click one of the four **Corners** buttons in the Control panel.

Muse applies the default radius (10) to the chosen corner.

7 To increase or decrease the corner radius, enter a value in the Control panel **Corners** field or click the neighboring up/down arrows.

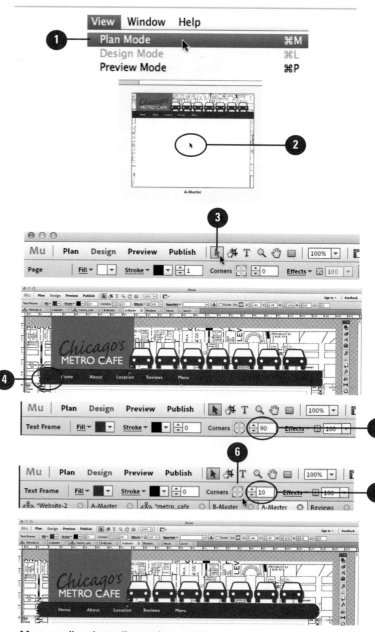

Muse applies the radius to the corners.

Applying a Drop Shadow

With Muse, it is not necessary to apply drop shadows to your graphics in a separate application, such as Photoshop, Fireworks, or Illustrator. You can apply this popular design effect to selected graphics directly in Muse by enabling the effect from the drop-down Effects panel. The panel also lets you choose familiar shadow options, such as color, opacity, size, angle, and distance.

Enable the shadow effect

1. Choose **Plan Mode** from the **View** menu.

   TIMESAVER *Press Cmd+M (Mac) or Ctrl+M (Win) to apply the Plan Mode command quickly.*

2. From the sitemap, double-click the thumbnail of the page whose object you'd like to apply an effect to.

   Muse opens the page in Design Mode.

3. Click the **Selection Tool** icon at the top of the Design Mode interface.

   TIMESAVER *Press V to access the Selection tool quickly.*

4. To select the object you'd like to apply an effect to, click it with the **Selection** tool.

5. Click the **Effects** button in the Control panel to display a drop-down Effects panel.

6. Click the **Shadow** button in the upper-left corner of the drop-down Effects panel.

7. Enable the effect by placing a check in the **On** checkbox.

8. Click the **Color Swatch** icon in the drop-down Effects panel.

   Muse displays a drop-down Color Picker.

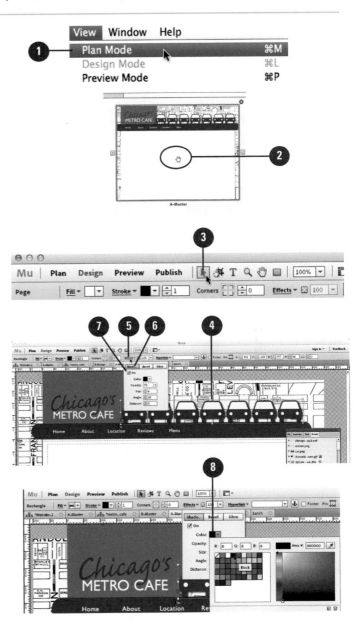

9. Choose a shadow color with the Color Picker via any of the following methods:

   ◆ Enter values into the **RGB** fields.

   ◆ Enter a hexadecimal code in the **Hex#** field.

   ◆ Click a **swatch** from the saved **color swatch list**.

   ◆ Drag the **Hue** slider up or down to select a color hue. Then click in the color field to the right of the Hue slider to determine the saturation and brightness of the selected color.

   ◆ Click the **Sample Color Tool** icon. To sample a color for the shadow, proceed to click anywhere on the page—including in a placed photo or graphic.

10. Enter a value in the **Opacity** field, or click and drag the drop-down **Opacity** slider.

11. Determine the softness/hardness of the shadow by entering a value in the **Size** field. Higher values produce softer shadows; lower values produce harder shadows.

12. Determine the angle of the shadow by entering a value in the **Angle** field.

13. Determine the shadow distance by entering a value in the **Distance** field.

14. Click away to close the drop-down Effects panel and view the effect.

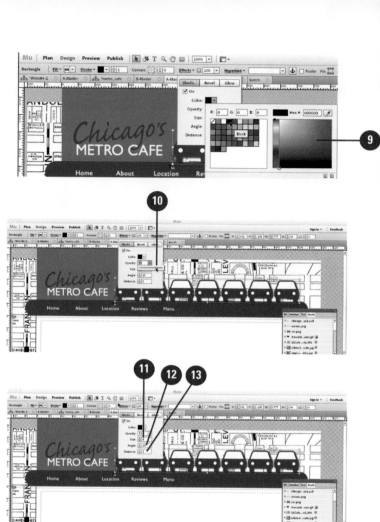

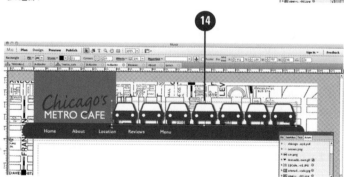

Applying a Bevel

A bevel effect creates the appearance of a sloped surface or edge. Bevel effects are often used to enhance buttons and other small web icons. As it is with drop shadows, you do not need to apply bevels using an outside application such as Photoshop, Fireworks, or Illustrator. You can apply bevels directly in Muse by selecting the graphic and enabling the option from the Effects panel. The panel also lets you choose familiar bevel options, such as opacity, size, angle, and distance.

Enable the bevel effect

① Choose **Plan Mode** from the **View** menu.

TIMESAVER *Press Cmd+M (Mac) or Ctrl+M (Win) to apply the Plan Mode command quickly.*

② From the sitemap, double-click the thumbnail of the page whose object you'd like to apply an effect to.

Muse opens the page in Design Mode.

③ Click the **Selection Tool** icon at the top of the Design Mode interface.

TIMESAVER *Press V to access the Selection tool quickly.*

④ To select the object you'd like to apply an effect to, click it with the **Selection** tool.

⑤ Click the **Effects** button in the Control panel to display a drop-down Effects panel.

⑥ Click the **Bevel** button in the upper portion of the drop-down Effects panel.

⑦ Enable the effect by placing a check in the **On** checkbox.

⑧ Enter a value in the **Opacity** field, or click and drag the drop-down **Opacity** slider.

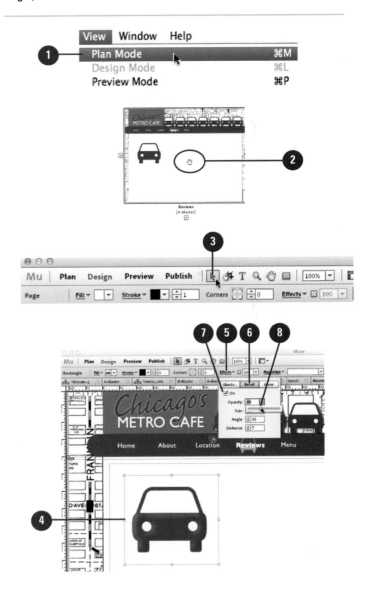

9. Determine the softness/hardness of the bevel by entering a value in the **Size** field. Higher values produce softer bevels; lower values produce harder bevels.

10. Determine the angle of the bevel by entering a value in the **Angle** field.

11. Determine the bevel depth by entering a value in the **Distance** field.

12. Click away to close the drop-down Effects panel and view the effect.

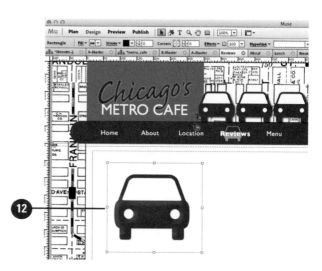

Applying a Glow

By applying a glow effect, you can help graphics and text objects "pop" off the page. They're great for making objects stand out over a busy or dark background. Just like with shadows and bevels, it is not necessary to apply glow effects using an outside application, such as Photoshop, Fireworks, or Illustrator. You can apply this effect directly in Muse by enabling it from the drop-down Effects panel. The panel also lets you choose familiar glow options, such as color, opacity, and size.

Enable the glow effect

1. Choose **Plan Mode** from the **View** menu.

   TIMESAVER *Press Cmd+M (Mac) or Ctrl+M (Win) to apply the Plan Mode command quickly.*

2. From the sitemap, double-click the thumbnail of the page whose object you'd like to apply an effect to.

   Muse opens the page in Design Mode.

3. Click the **Selection Tool** icon at the top of the Design Mode interface.

   TIMESAVER *Press V to access the Selection tool quickly.*

4. To select the object you'd like to apply an effect to, click it with the **Selection** tool.

5. Click the **Effects** button in the Control panel to display a drop-down Effects panel.

6. Click the **Glow** button in the upper-right corner of the drop-down Effects panel.

7. Enable the effect by placing a check in the **On** checkbox.

8. Click the **Color Swatch** icon in the drop-down Effects panel.

   Muse displays a drop-down Color Picker.

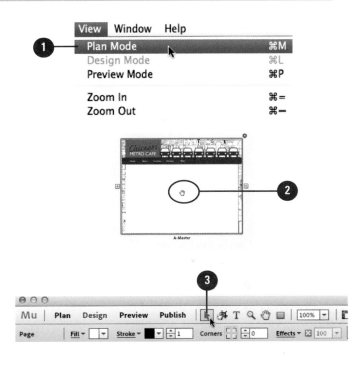

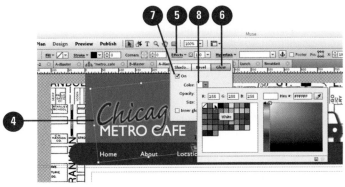

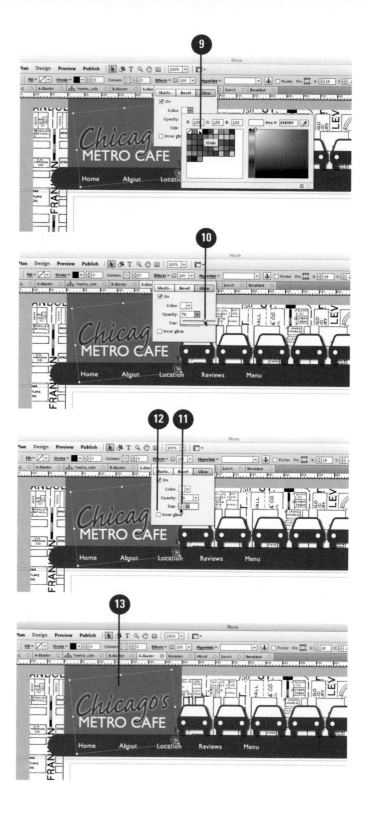

9 Choose a shadow color with the Color Picker via any of the following methods:

- ◆ Enter values into the **RGB** fields.

- ◆ Enter a hexadecimal code in the **Hex#** field.

- ◆ Click a **swatch** from the saved **color swatch list**.

- ◆ Drag the **Hue** slider up or down to select a color hue. Then click in the color field to the right of the Hue slider to determine the saturation and brightness of the selected color.

- ◆ Click the **Sample Color Tool** icon. To sample a color for the shadow, proceed to click anywhere on the page—including in a placed photo or graphic.

10 Enter a value in the **Opacity** field, or click and drag the drop-down **Opacity** slider.

11 Determine the softness/hardness of the glow by entering a value in the **Size** field. Higher values produce softer glows; lower values produce harder glows.

12 By default, Muse applies an outer glow effect. To create an inner glow effect, enable the **Inner Glow** option in the drop-down Effects panel.

13 Click away to close the drop-down Effects panel and view the effect.

Changing Opacity

With Muse, you can adjust the opacity of any object on a page, including rectangles with a fill color applied, placed graphics, and editable text objects. By default the opacity setting for all objects is 100% (completely opaque). Lowering a selected object's opacity setting enables you to see through it to the objects underneath. To change an object's opacity, enter a precentage value in the Opacity field of the Control panel.

Enter a percentage in the opacity field

1 Choose **Plan Mode** from the **View** menu.

TIMESAVER *Press Cmd+M (Mac) or Ctrl+M (Win) to apply the Plan Mode command quickly.*

2 From the sitemap, double-click the thumbnail of the page whose object you'd like to adjust.

Muse opens the page in Design Mode.

3 Click the **Selection Tool** icon at the top of the Design Mode interface.

TIMESAVER *Press V to access the Selection tool quickly.*

4 Select the object by clicking it with the **Selection** tool.

5 Enter a percentage in the Control panel **Opacity** field.

Muse applies the opacity setting to the selected object.

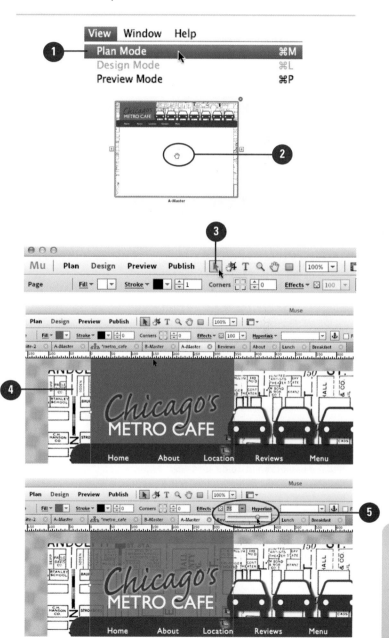

Saving a Graphic Style

Graphic styles enable you to save your favorite combinations of object attributes, such as fill and stroke color, wrap offset and alignment, drop shadows, bevels, glows, and more. After you save a graphic style, you can apply the attributes to a selected object with a single click of the mouse. You can create a graphic style by selecting an object that already has the attributes applied and clicking the new style button located at the bottom of the Graphic Styles panel.

Click the Create a New Style from Applied Attributes button

1. Choose **Plan Mode** from the **View** menu.

   TIMESAVER *Press Cmd+M (Mac) or Ctrl+M (Win) to apply the Plan Mode command quickly.*

2. From the sitemap, double-click the thumbnail of a page whose objects contain attributes you'd like to save as a graphic style.

   Muse opens the page in Design Mode.

3. Click the **Selection Tool** icon at the top of the Design Mode interface.

   TIMESAVER *Press V to access the Selection tool quickly.*

4. To display the Graphic Styles panel, choose **Window > Graphic Styles**.

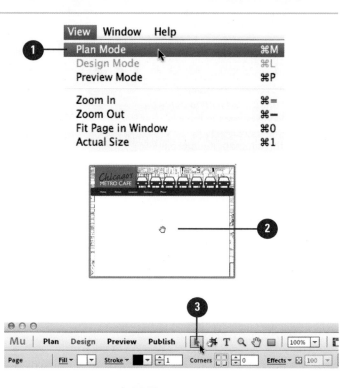

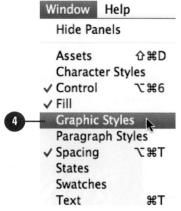

Did You Know?

You can unlink an object from its applied graphic style. To do so, select the object with the Selection tool. Muse highlights the name of the applied style in the Graphic Styles panel. To unlink the object from the style, click the Unlink Style button located at the bottom of the panel.

5 Select the object by clicking it with the **Selection** tool.

6 Click the **Create a New Style from Applied Attributes** button, located at the bottom of the Graphic Styles panel.

Muse saves the attributes currently applied to the selected graphic as a style. By default, Muse names the new style, **Style 1**.

7 To rename the style, access the contextual menu by right-clicking or Control-clicking (Mac) **Style 1** in the Graphic Styles panel and choose **Rename Style**.

Muse highlights the style name in the Graphic Styles panel.

IMPORTANT *Always use the contextual menu to rename or edit style options. Double-clicking the style name in the Graphic Styles panel applies the style to the currently selected object. If no objects are selected, Muse applies the style to the entire page.*

8 Enter a name for the style and press Return (Mac) or Enter (Win).

Muse applies the new style name.

Did You Know?

The plus symbol means there is a style override. When you see a plus symbol (+) next to a style name in the Graphic Styles panel, this indicates that additional attributes—that are not part of the stlye—have been applied to the object.

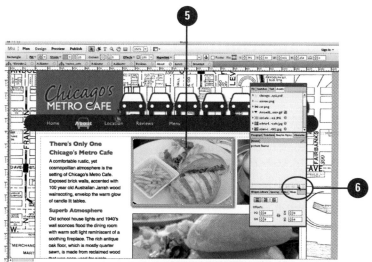

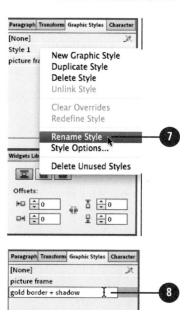

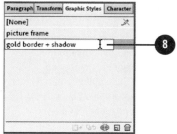

Applying a Graphic Style

Applying graphic styles in Muse is just as easy as creating them. After you save your favorite object attributes as a graphic style, you can apply them to a selected object by clicking the style name in the Graphic Styles panel. Any additional attributes that you apply to an object after applying the graphic style are considered overrides. You can clear style overrides by Option-(Mac) or Alt-(Win) clicking the style name in the Graphic Styles panel or by clicking the Clear Overrides button located at the bottom of the panel.

Click the style name in the Graphic Styles panel

1. Choose **Plan Mode** from the **View** menu.

   TIMESAVER *Press Cmd+M (Mac) or Ctrl+M (Win) to apply the Plan Mode command quickly.*

2. From the sitemap, double-click the thumbnail of a page whose objects you'd like to apply a graphic style to.

   Muse opens the page in Design Mode.

3. Click the **Selection Tool** icon at the top of the Design Mode interface.

4. To display the Graphic Styles panel, choose **Window > Graphic Styles**.

Did You Know?

The only way to edit a graphic style is to redefine it. To add overrides to the style definition, select the object and click the Redefine Style button located at the bottom of the Graphic Styles panel (it's the second icon from the left), or choose the command from the contextual menu.

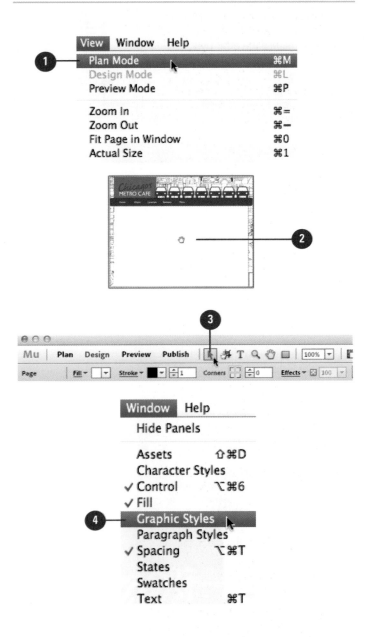

5 Select the object by clicking it with the **Selection** tool.

6 Click the style name in the Graphic Styles panel.

Muse applies the saved graphic style attributes to the selected object.

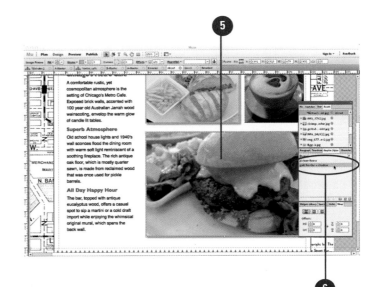

Deleting a Graphic Style

To delete a style from the Graphic Styles panel, hover the cursor over the style name in the panel and right-click or Control-click (Mac) to access the contextual menu. Choose Delete Style to remove the style from the panel. If the style you are deleting is currently applied to any objects in the site, Muse asks you what style you would like to use to replace it. Choose a replacement style from the Replace Style list and click Replace.

Choose the Delete Style command

1. Choose **Design Mode** from the **View** menu.

   TIMESAVER *Press Cmd+L (Mac) or Ctrl+L (Win) to apply the Design Mode command quickly.*

   Muse opens the current page in Design Mode.

2. To display the Graphic Styles panel, choose **Window > Graphic Styles**.

3. Access the contextual menu by right-clicking or Control-clicking (Mac) the style name in the Graphic Styles panel, and choose **Delete Style**.

   If the style is being used anywhere in the site, Muse displays the Replace Style window.

4. Select a style from the **Replace Style** list.

5. Click **Replace**.

   Any objects that were stylized by the now deleted style assume the attributes of the replacement style.

   IMPORTANT *To replace a style with no style, choose None from the Replace Style list. When you do, Muse retains the applied style attributes.*

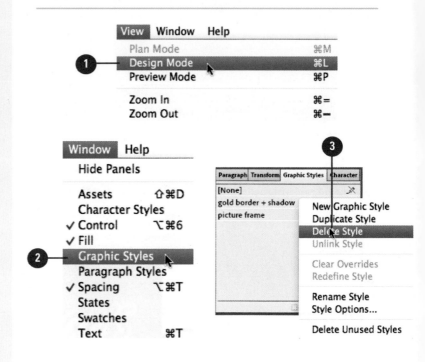

Working with Text

7

Introduction

Working with text in Muse is very similar to working with text in Adobe InDesign and Illustrator. If you're a designer who is already familiar with formatting text in these Creative Suite applications, then you'll feel right at home with formatting text in Muse.

In this chapter, you'll learn how to import text into a layout using the Place command, as well as by copying and pasting it from other applications, such as Microsoft Word, or even Adobe InDesign. You'll also learn how to select individual text characters with the Text tool.

This chapter also explains how to apply formatting attributes to text. This includes character attributes, such as font size, style options (bold, italic, underline), text alignment, color, and letter spacing. It also includes paragraph attributes, such as leading, paragraph indents, margin spacing, and spacing before and after.

You'll also learn the difference between applying web safe fonts and system fonts to your text. Muse makes it easy for you to apply browser-friendly fonts to your body text, but you also have access to all other fonts loaded on your system.

Importing Text by Copying and Pasting

One of the easiest ways to import text into a layout is by copying and pasting it from a separate application, such as Microsoft Word, Adobe InDesign, or even a web browser. To do so, open the file in its native application and copy it to the Clipboard. When you return to Muse, choose the Paste command from the Edit menu. Muse automatically places the copied text into a frame and applies default character and paragraph formatting.

Copy text to the Clipboard

1. Choose **Plan Mode** from the **View** menu.

    TIMESAVER *Press Cmd+M (Mac) or Ctrl+M (Win) to apply the Plan Mode command quickly.*

2. Double-click any page or master page thumbnail from the sitemap.

    Muse opens the page in Design Mode.

3. Select the text from its native application, such as a Microsoft Word, Adobe InDesign, or even a website displayed in your default browser.

4. Copy the text to the Clipboard by choosing **Edit > Copy**.

    TIMESAVER *Press Cmd+C (Mac) or Ctrl+C (Win) to apply the Copy command quickly.*

5. Paste the text into the Muse layout by choosing **Edit > Paste**.

    TIMESAVER *Press Cmd+V (Mac) or Ctrl+V (Win) to apply the Paste command quickly.*

    Muse automatically creates a text frame and places the copied text using default character and paragraph formatting.

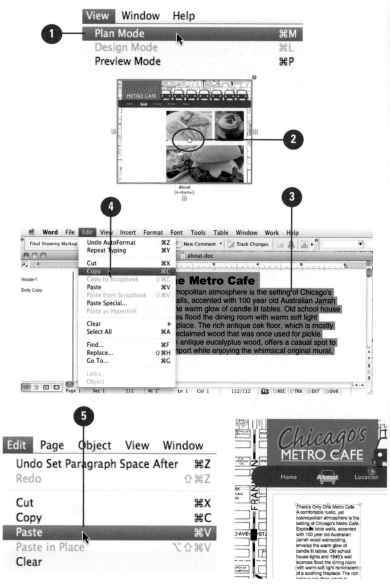

Muse pastes the text using default formatting.

Placing Text

Another way to import text into your layouts is by using the Place command. Just as you can use the Place command to import graphics, you can also use it to import text. However, in order to do so, the text must be saved in the .TXT format—not .RTF (Real Text format) or .DOC (Microsoft Word document). After you select the .TXT file with the Import dialog box, click the loaded place cursor anywhere on the page. Muse automatically creates a text frame and places the text with default character and paragraph formatting applied.

Choose the Place command

1. Choose **Plan Mode** from the **View** menu.

   TIMESAVER *Press Cmd+M (Mac) or Ctrl+M (Win) to apply the Plan Mode command quickly.*

2. Double-click any page or master page thumbnail from the sitemap.

   Muse opens the page in Design Mode.

3. Choose **File > Place** to access the Import dialog box.

4. Using the Import dialog box, navigate to the .TXT file on your system disk. Click the .TXT file to select it.

5. Click **Select**.

   IMPORTANT *You can only import text files saved in the .TXT file format, not Microsoft Word (.DOC) or Real Text (.RTF).*

6. Click the loaded place cursor anywhere on the page to place the text.

   Muse automatically creates a text frame and places the text using default character and paragraph formatting.

Muse places the text using default formatting.

Selecting Text

To apply formatting to all of the text in a frame, you can select the frame with the Selection tool and then apply the attributes. However, if you'd like to apply formatting to specific characters within the frame, then you must first highlight those characters with the Text tool. To do so, click and drag over the characters with the tool, and then apply the formatting attributes.

Highlight text with the Text tool

1. Choose **Plan Mode** from the **View** menu.

   TIMESAVER *Press Cmd+M (Mac) or Ctrl+M (Win) to apply the Plan Mode command quickly.*

2. From the sitemap, double-click the thumbnail of a page containing text you'd like to select.

   Muse opens the page in Design Mode.

3. Click the **Text Tool** icon at the top of the Design Mode interface.

   TIMESAVER *Press T to access the Text tool quickly.*

4. Click and drag over the text characters with the Text tool cursor.

   Muse highlights the characters as you drag to let you know they are now selected.

Choosing a Web Safe Font

The Font list in Muse is broken up into two sections: web safe fonts and system fonts. Web safe fonts are accessible across both platforms (Mac and Windows) and will load in any browser. System fonts are the fonts you currently have activated on your system. These fonts are not web safe. As a result, Muse converts them to graphics when you export the site. Web safe fonts are best used for body copy throughout your layouts.

Choose a web safe font from the Font list

1 Choose **Plan Mode** from the **View** menu.

> **TIMESAVER** *Press Cmd+M (Mac) or Ctrl+M (Win) to apply the Plan Mode command quickly.*

2 From the sitemap, double-click the thumbnail of a page you'd like to add web safe text to.

> Muse opens the page in Design Mode.

3 Click the **Text Tool** icon at the top of the Design Mode interface.

> **TIMESAVER** *Press T to access the Text tool quickly.*

4 Click and drag over some existing text characters with the Text tool cursor.

5 Choose a web safe font from the **Font** list in the Control panel or Text panel.

> **IMPORTANT** *Web safe fonts always appear at the top of the Font list. Muse also displays a globe icon next to the chosen font to let you know that it is web safe. If you do not see the globe icon, then you have chosen a system font. Muse converts all system fonts into graphics when you export the site.*

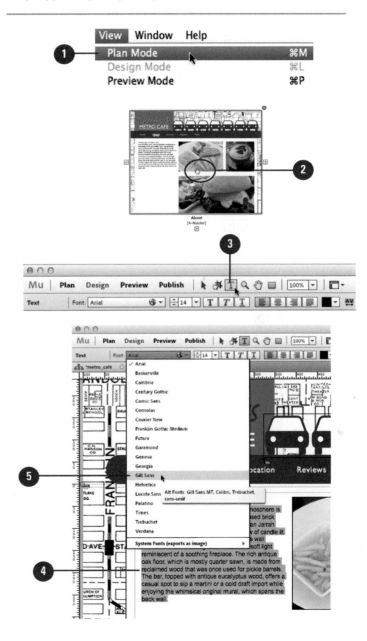

Choosing a System Font

Choose a system font from the Font list

1. Choose **Plan Mode** from the **View** menu.

    TIMESAVER *Press Cmd+M (Mac) or Ctrl+M (Win) to apply the Plan Mode command quickly.*

2. From the sitemap, double-click the thumbnail of a page you'd like to add text to.

    Muse opens the page in Design Mode.

3. Click the **Text Tool** icon at the top of the Design Mode interface.

    TIMESAVER *Press T to access the Text tool quickly.*

4. Click and drag over some existing text characters with the Text tool cursor.

5. Choose a system font from the **Font** list in the Control panel or Text panel.

    IMPORTANT *System fonts always appear at the bottom of the Font list and are not web safe. If you do not see the globe icon next to the font name in the Control panel, then you have chosen a system font. Muse converts all system fonts into graphics when you export the site. As a result, the more system fonts you use, the longer it will take for the page to load in a browser.*

System fonts are the fonts you currently have activated on your system. They always appear at the bottom of the Font list and are not web safe. This means that they are not accessible across both platforms (Mac and Windows) and will not load in every browser. Because of this, Muse converts them to graphics when you export the site. Whenever you use a system font, Muse displays a system font icon in the bottom-right corner of the text frame to remind you that the text will be exported as a graphic. System fonts are best used for text objects that also serve as graphic elements in your site design.

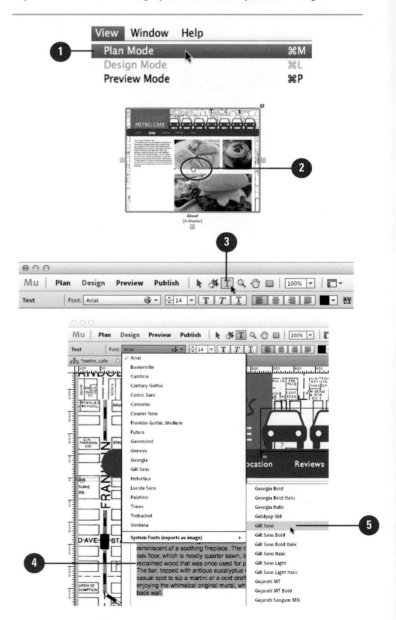

Changing Text Size

Enter a value in the Size field

1. Choose **Plan Mode** from the **View** menu.

   TIMESAVER *Press Cmd+M (Mac) or Ctrl+M (Win) to apply the Plan Mode command quickly.*

2. From the sitemap, double-click the thumbnail of the page containing text you'd like to edit.

   Muse opens the page in Design Mode.

3. Click the **Selection Tool** icon at the top of the Design Mode interface.

4. Select the text frame by clicking it with the **Selection** tool.

5. Click the **Text Tool** icon at the top of the Design Mode interface.

6. Click and drag over some existing text characters with the Text tool cursor.

7. Enter a size for the text in the **Size** field of the Control panel or Text panel.

   Muse applies the new size setting to the selected text.

Did You Know?

You can also adjust text size with keyboard shortcuts. To adjust the text size in 2-point increments, select the text and press Cmd+Shift+>/< (Mac) or Ctrl+Shift+>/< (Win). The greater than key increases the point size; the lesser than key decreases the point size.

The Size field in the Control panel (and Text panel) enables you to specify how small or large you would like text objects to appear in your layout. To adjust the size of the text, select the text object or individual text characters, and enter a value in the Size field. You can also adjust the size value in 1-point increments by clicking the up/down arrows to the left of the Size field, or choose a preset size from the drop-down list.

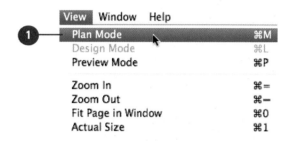

Applying Bold, Italic, and Underline Attributes

The font style buttons located in the Control panel (and Text panel) enable you to apply a bold, italic, and underline effect to selected text objects. These options are best used with web safe fonts to add emphasis to certain words within a larger body of text. They are also useful for creating hyperlink styles (see Chapter 9 "Adding Hyperlinks") and menu rollover states (see Chapter 4 "Adding Navigational Content").

Click the font style buttons

1 Choose **Plan Mode** from the **View** menu.

TIMESAVER *Press Cmd+M (Mac) or Ctrl+M (Win) to apply the Plan Mode command quickly.*

2 From the sitemap, double-click the thumbnail of the page containing text you'd like to edit.

Muse opens the page in Design Mode.

3 Click the **Selection Tool** icon at the top of the Design Mode interface.

TIMESAVER *Press V to access the Selection tool quickly.*

4 Select the text frame by clicking it with the **Selection** tool.

5 Click the **Text Tool** icon at the top of the Design Mode interface.

TIMESAVER *Press T to access the Text tool quickly.*

6 Click and drag over some existing text characters with the Text tool cursor.

7 Click the **Bold**, **Italic**, or **Underline** buttons in the Control panel or Text panel.

Muse applies the new style setting to the selected text.

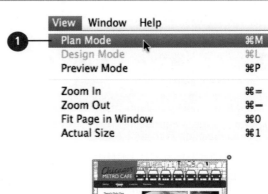

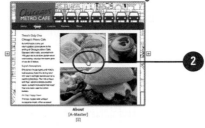

Changing Text Alignment

By clicking the text Alignment buttons located in the Control panel or Text panel, you can specify how the selected paragraphs should be aligned. Options include Align Left (flush left/ragged right), Align Center (ragged left and right), Align Right (flush right/ragged left), and Align Justify (flush left and right). You can also change text alignment by using keyboard shortcuts. To do so, select the text and press Cmd+Shift+R (Mac) or Ctrl+Shift+R (Win) to align right; press Cmd+Shift+L (Mac) or Ctrl+Shift+L (Win) to align left; press Cmd+Shift+C (Mac) or Ctrl+Shift+C (Win) to align center.

Click the Alignment buttons

1. Choose **Plan Mode** from the **View** menu.

   TIMESAVER *Press Cmd+M (Mac) or Ctrl+M (Win) to apply the Plan Mode command quickly.*

2. From the sitemap, double-click the thumbnail of the page containing text you'd like to edit.

   Muse opens the page in Design Mode.

3. Click the **Selection Tool** icon at the top of the Design Mode interface.

   TIMESAVER *Press V to access the Selection tool quickly.*

4. Select the text frame by clicking it with the **Selection** tool.

5. Click the **Text Tool** icon at the top of the Design Mode interface.

   TIMESAVER *Press T to access the Text tool quickly.*

6. To apply an alignment option, click one of the **Alignment** buttons in the Control panel or Text panel. Options include: **Align Left**, **Align Center**, **Align Right**, and **Align Justify**.

   Muse applies the new alignment setting to the selected text.

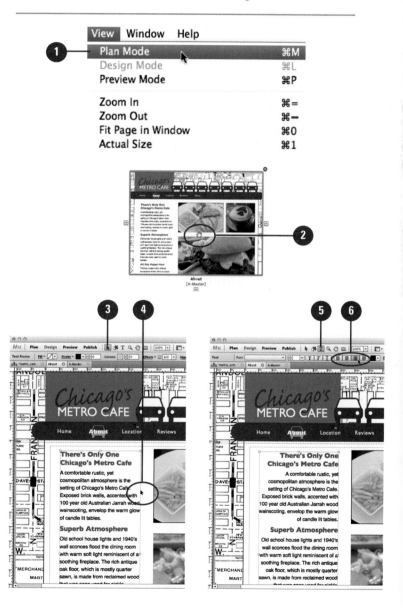

Changing Text Color

Not only can you use the Color Picker to apply fill and stroke colors to rectangles, but you can also use it to colorize selected text. To access the Color Picker as a flyout window, click the Text Color swatch located in the Control panel or Text panel. The default text color is black, but you can apply a different color in several different ways using the Color Picker. You can choose a preset color swatch, drag the Hue slider and click in the color field, enter a hexadecimal code, enter values in the RGB field, or use the Sample Color tool to access a color from anywhere on the page.

Choose a text color with the Color Picker

1. Choose **Plan Mode** from the **View** menu.

   TIMESAVER *Press Cmd+M (Mac) or Ctrl+M (Win) to apply the Plan Mode command quickly.*

2. From the sitemap, double-click the thumbnail of the page containing text you'd like to edit.

   Muse opens the page in Design Mode.

3. Click the **Selection Tool** icon at the top of the Design Mode interface.

   TIMESAVER *Press V to access the Selection tool quickly.*

4. Select the text frame by clicking it with the Selection tool.

5. Click the **Text Tool** icon at the top of the Design Mode interface.

   TIMESAVER *Press T to access the Text tool quickly.*

6. Click and drag over some existing text characters with the Text tool cursor.

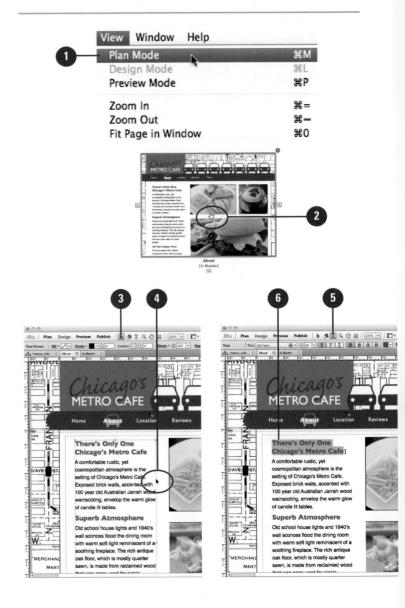

7 Choose a text color with the Color Picker via any of the following methods:

◆ Enter values into the **RGB** fields.

◆ Enter a hexadecimal code in the **Hex#** field.

◆ Click a **swatch** from the saved **color swatch list**.

◆ Drag the **Hue** slider up or down to select a color hue. Then click in the color field to the right of the Hue slider to determine the saturation and brightness of the selected color.

◆ Click the **Sample Color Tool** icon. To sample a color for the text, proceed to click anywhere on the page—including in a placed photo or graphic.

Click away to apply the new text color.

Muse applies the new text color to the selected text.

Muse applies the new text color to the selected text.

Changing Letter Spacing

You can adjust letter spacing, also referred to as kerning, by entering a value in the Letter Space field of the Control panel or Text panel. The default letter spacing value is zero. By entering positive values, you can spread the letters further apart. By entering negative values, you can bring them closer together. You can also change the letter spacing between two specific characters by placing the Text tool cursor between them and entering a value in the Letter Space field. Note that adjusting letter spacing adds a significant amount of code to your site. The more letter spacing you apply, the longer it will take for the page to load into a browser.

Enter a value in the Letter Space field

① Choose **Plan Mode** from the **View** menu.

TIMESAVER *Press Cmd+M (Mac) or Ctrl+M (Win) to apply the Plan Mode command quickly.*

② From the sitemap, double-click the thumbnail of the page containing text you'd like to edit.

Muse opens the page in Design Mode.

③ Click the **Selection Tool** icon at the top of the Design Mode interface.

④ Select the text frame by clicking it with the **Selection** tool.

⑤ Click the **Text Tool** icon at the top of the Design Mode interface.

⑥ Enter a spacing value for the text in the **Letter Space** field of the Control panel or Text panel.

Muse applies the new letter spacing to the selected text.

Did You Know?

You can also adjust letter spacing with keyboard shortcuts. To adjust letter spacing in 1-point increments, place the Text tool cursor between the characters and press Option-left/right arrow key (Mac) or Alt-left/right arrow key (Win). The left arrow key brings the characters closer together; the right arrow key moves them further apart.

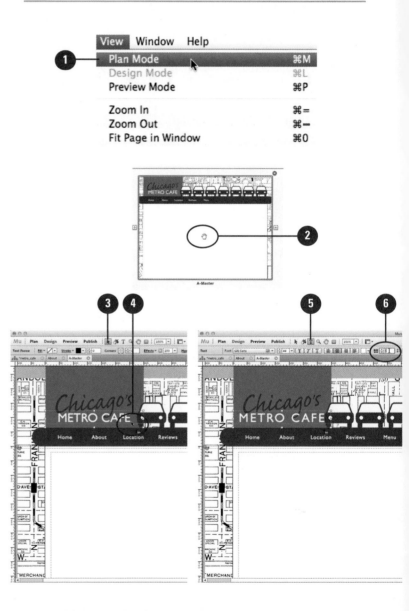

Changing Leading

You can adjust the amount of space between lines of a paragraph, also referred to as leading, by entering a percentage value in the Leading field of the Control panel or Text panel. The default leading value is 120%. By entering higher values, you can increase the space between lines; by entering lower values, you can decrease it. You can also adjust the leading value in 1-point increments by clicking the up/down arrows to the left of the Leading field.

Enter a value in the Leading field

1. Choose **Plan Mode** from the **View** menu.

   TIMESAVER *Press Cmd+M (Mac) or Ctrl+M (Win) to apply the Plan Mode command quickly.*

2. From the sitemap, double-click the thumbnail of the page containing text you'd like to edit.

   Muse opens the page in Design Mode.

3. Click the **Selection Tool** icon at the top of the Design Mode interface.

4. Select the text frame by clicking it with the **Selection** tool.

5. Click the **Text Tool** icon at the top of the Design Mode interface.

6. Click and drag over some existing text characters with the Text tool cursor.

7. Enter a leading value for the text in the **Leading** field of the Control panel or Text panel.

   Muse applies the new leading value to the selected text.

Did You Know?

You can also adjust leading with keyboard shortcuts. To adjust the text size in 2-point increments, select the text and press Option-up/down arrow key (Mac) or Alt-up/down arrow key (Win). The down arrow key brings the lines closer together; the up arrow key moves them further apart.

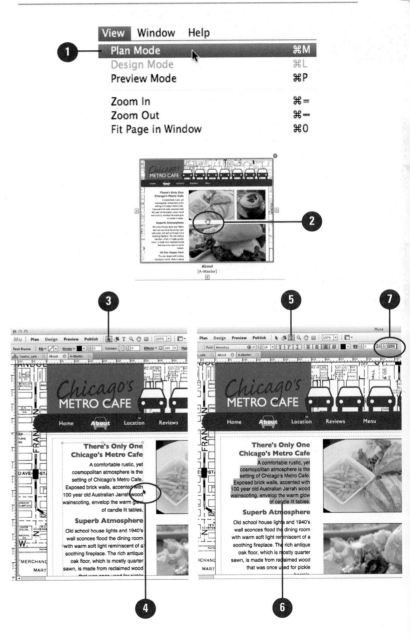

Inserting a Paragraph Indent

You can place an indent on the first line of a paragraph by selecting the text object and entering a value in the Indent field of the Text panel. The default indent value is zero (no indent). By entering positive values, you can indent the first line of the paragraph inward (to the right); by entering negative values, you can indent the first line outward (to the left). You can also adjust the indent value in 1-point increments by clicking the up/down arrows to the left of the Indent field.

Enter a value in the Indent field

1. Choose **Plan Mode** from the **View** menu.

   TIMESAVER Press Cmd+M (Mac) or Ctrl+M (Win) to apply the Plan Mode command quickly.

2. From the sitemap, double-click the thumbnail of the page containing text you'd like to edit.

   Muse opens the page in Design Mode.

3. Click the **Selection Tool** icon at the top of the Design Mode interface.

   TIMESAVER Press V to access the Selection tool quickly.

4. Select the text frame by clicking it with the **Selection** tool.

5. Click the **Text Tool** icon at the top of the Design Mode interface.

   TIMESAVER Press T to access the Text tool quickly.

6. Insert the Text tool cursor in the paragraph you would like to indent.

7. Choose **Window > Text** to display the Text panel.

8. Enter a value for the paragraph indent in the **Indent** field of the Text panel.

   Muse applies the paragraph indent to the selected text.

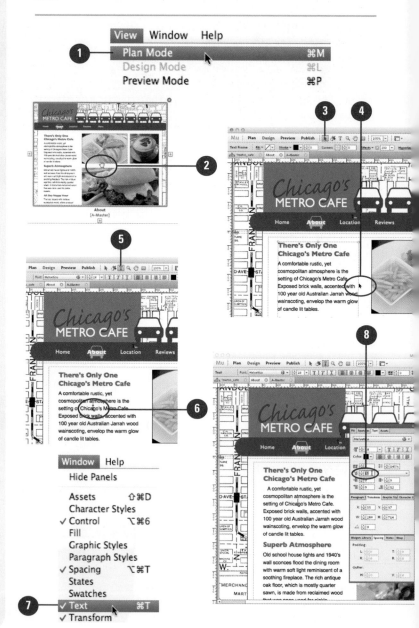

Inserting Left and Right Margins

You can add space on either side of a paragraph by selecting the text object and entering a value in the Left Margin and Right Margin fields of the Text panel. The default margin values are zero (no margin). By entering positive values in the Left Margin field, you can move all lines of the paragraph inward (to the right); by entering negative values, you can move all lines outward (to the left). The opposite occurs when entering positive and negative values in the Right Margin field. You can also adjust the margin values in 1-point increments by clicking the up/down arrows to the left of the Margin fields.

Enter a value in the Left Margin/Right Margin field

1. Choose **Plan Mode** from the **View** menu.

   TIMESAVER *Press Cmd+M (Mac) or Ctrl+M (Win) to apply the Plan Mode command quickly.*

2. From the sitemap, double-click the thumbnail of the page containing text you'd like to edit.

   Muse opens the page in Design Mode.

3. Click the **Selection Tool** icon at the top of the Design Mode interface.

   TIMESAVER *Press V to access the Selection tool quickly.*

4. Select the text frame by clicking it with the **Selection** tool.

5. Choose **Window > Text** to display the Text panel.

6. Enter a value for the margin in the **Left Margin** or **Right Margin** field of the Text panel.

   Muse applies the margin spacing to the selected text.

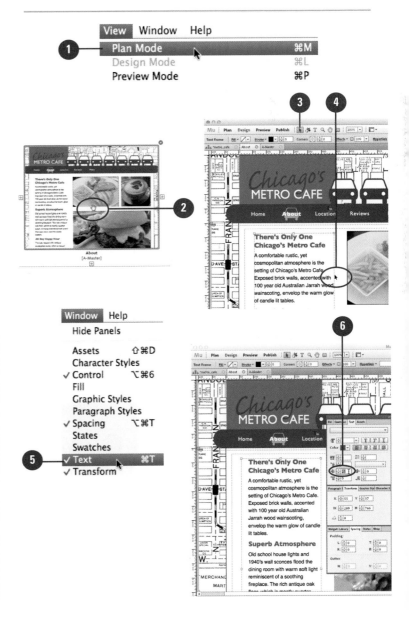

Adding Space Before and After a Paragraph

You can add space above and below a paragraph by selecting the text object and entering a value in the Space Before and Space After fields of the Text panel. The default values are zero (no extra space). By entering positive values in either field, you can add space above and below the paragraph. You can also adjust the spacing values in 1-point increments by clicking the up/down arrows to the left of either field.

Enter a value in the Space Before/Space After fields

1. Choose **Plan Mode** from the **View** menu.

   TIMESAVER *Press Cmd+M (Mac) or Ctrl+M (Win) to apply the Plan Mode command quickly.*

2. From the sitemap, double-click the thumbnail of the page containing text you'd like to edit.

   Muse opens the page in Design Mode.

3. Click the **Selection Tool** icon at the top of the Design Mode interface.

   TIMESAVER *Press V to access the Selection tool quickly.*

4. Select the text frame by clicking it with the **Selection** tool.

5. Choose **Window > Text** to display the Text panel.

6. Enter a spacing value in the **Space Before** of **Space After** field of the Text panel.

   Muse applies the spacing to the selected text.

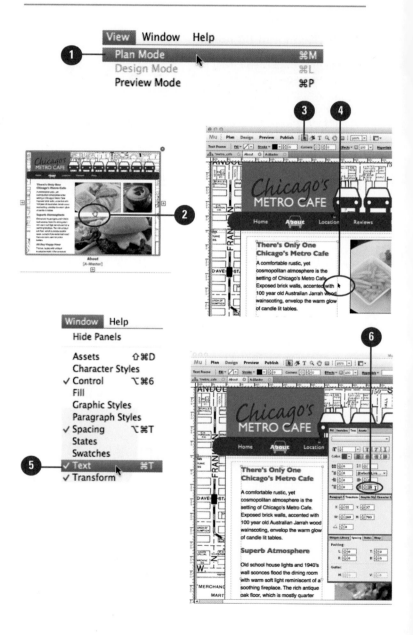

Working with Character and Paragraph Styles

8

Introduction

Styles enable you to save your favorite combinations of text formatting attributes. You can then apply these attributes to other text objects with a single click. With character styles you can save character attributes, such as font size, style options (bold, italic, underline), text alignment, and text color. With paragraph styles, you can include character attributes as well as paragraph attributes, including leading, paragraph indents, margin spacing, and spacing before and after.

With this chapter, you'll learn how to save and apply both character styles and paragraph styles. You'll also learn how to apply formatting overrides to stylized text, as well as how to remove them. In addition, you'll learn how to redefine styles to include any formatting overrides you've applied.

This chapter also explains how to unlink styles from any text objects you've applied styles to, and how to utilize space and paragraph tags by applying them via the Style Options dialog box.

Saving a
Character Style

Character styles enable you to save your favorite combinations of character formatting attributes, such as character color, style options (bold, italic, and underline), kerning, font, and font size. After you save a character style, you can apply all the saved attributes to a selected text object with a single click of the mouse. You can create a character style by selecting a text object that already has the attributes applied and then clicking the new style button located at the bottom of the Character Styles panel.

Click the Create a New Style from Applied Attributes button

1. Choose **Plan Mode** from the **View** menu.

   TIMESAVER *Press Cmd+M (Mac) or Ctrl+M (Win) to apply the Plan Mode command quickly.*

2. From the sitemap, double-click the thumbnail of a page whose text objects contain attributes you'd like to save as a character style.

   Muse opens the page in Design Mode.

3. Click the **Text Tool** icon at the top of the Design Mode interface.

   TIMESAVER *Press T to access the Text tool quickly.*

4. To display the Character Styles panel, choose **Window > Character Styles**.

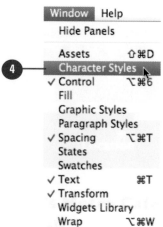

Did You Know?

Muse does not automatically apply the new character style to the object you created it from. To apply the character style to the object, you must select it and choose the style name from the Character Styles panel.

⑤ Click and drag over the formatted text characters with the Text tool cursor.

⑥ Click the **Create a New Style from Applied Attributes** button, located at the bottom of the Character Styles panel.

Muse saves the text attributes currently applied to the selected text object as a character style. By default, Muse names the new style **Character Style**.

⑦ To rename the style, access the contextual menu by right-clicking or Control-clicking (Mac) **Character Style** in the Character Styles panel and choose **Rename Style**.

Muse highlights the style name in the Character Styles panel.

IMPORTANT *Always use the contextual menu to rename or edit character style options. Double-clicking the style name in the Character Styles panel not only opens the Style Options dialog box, but also applies the style to the currently selected text object, which you may not want to do.*

⑧ Enter a name for the style and press Return (Mac) or Enter (Win).

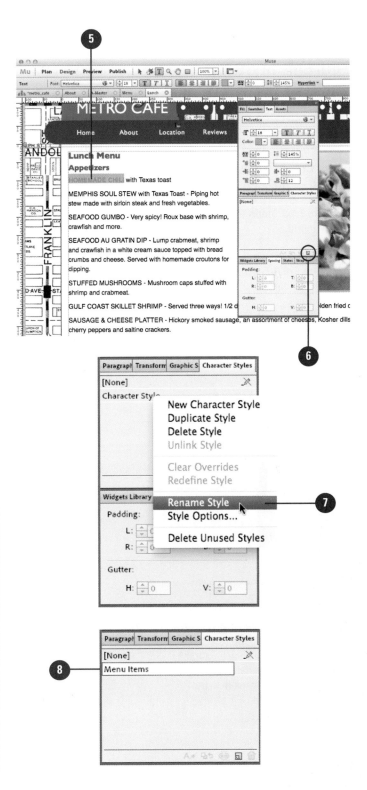

Did You Know?

Muse only saves character attributes that are not already applied as part of a paragraph style. If the text object you are basing a character style from already has a paragraph style applied, only those character attributes that are different from the paragraph style are saved as the new character style.

Saving a
Paragraph Style

Paragraph styles enable you to save your favorite combinations of character and paragraph formatting attributes. Every character attribute you can save as part of a character style can also be saved as part of a paragraph style. However, paragraph attributes, such as alignment and leading, can only be saved as part of a paragraph style. After you save a paragraph style, you can apply all the saved attributes to a selected text object with a single click of the mouse. You can create a paragraph style by selecting a text object that already has the attributes applied and then clicking the new style button located at the bottom of the Paragraph Styles panel.

Click the Create a New Style from Applied Attributes button

1. Choose **Plan Mode** from the **View** menu.

    TIMESAVER *Press Cmd+M (Mac) or Ctrl+M (Win) to apply the Plan Mode command quickly.*

2. From the sitemap, double-click the thumbnail of a page whose text objects contain attributes you'd like to save as a paragraph style.

    Muse opens the page in Design Mode.

3. Click the **Text Tool** icon at the top of the Design Mode interface.

    TIMESAVER *Press T to access the Text tool quickly.*

4. To display the Paragraph Styles panel, choose **Window > Paragraph Styles**.

Did You Know?

Muse does not automatically apply the new paragraph style to the object you created it from. To apply the paragraph style to the object, you must select it and choose the style name from the Paragraph Styles panel.

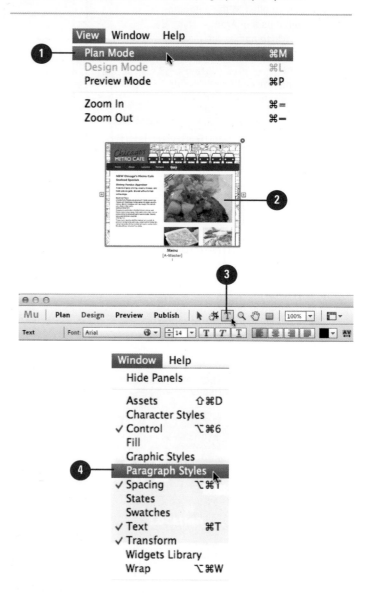

⑤ Click and drag over the formatted text characters with the Text tool cursor.

⑥ Click the **Create a New Style from Applied Attributes** button, located at the bottom of the Paragraph Styles panel.

Muse saves the text attributes currently applied to the selected text object as a paragraph style. By default, Muse names the new style **Paragraph Style**.

⑦ To rename the style, access the contextual menu by right-clicking or Control-clicking (Mac) **Paragraph Style** in the Paragraph Styles panel and choose **Rename Style**.

Muse highlights the style name in the Paragraph Styles panel.

IMPORTANT *Always use the contextual menu to rename or edit paragraph style options. Double-clicking the style name in the Paragraph Styles panel not only opens the Style Options dialog box, but also applies the style to the currently selected text object, which you may not want to do.*

⑧ Enter a name for the style and press Return (Mac) or Enter (Win).

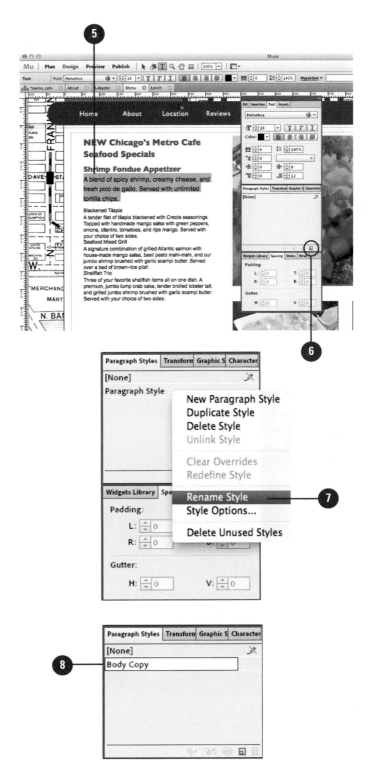

Applying a Character Style

Applying character styles in Muse is just as easy as creating them. After you save your favorite character attributes as a style, you can apply them to a selected text object by clicking the style name in the Character Styles panel. Character styles do not include paragraph formatting attributes, such as leading and alignment. They are best used for stylizing text items such as drop caps or single lines of text that you'd like to stand out from the rest of a paragraph.

Click the style name in the Character Styles panel

1. Choose **Plan Mode** from the **View** menu.

   TIMESAVER *Press Cmd+M (Mac) or Ctrl+M (Win) to apply the Plan Mode command quickly.*

2. From the sitemap, double-click the thumbnail of a page whose text objects you'd like to apply a character style to.

   Muse opens the page in Design Mode.

3. Click the **Text Tool** icon at the top of the Design Mode interface.

   TIMESAVER *Press T to access the Text tool quickly.*

4. To display the Character Styles panel, choose **Window > Character Styles**.

Did You Know?

You can apply a character style to a text object that has a paragraph style applied. When you apply a character style to a text object that already has a paragraph style applied, Muse applies the character style definition and does not treat it as a paragraph style override.

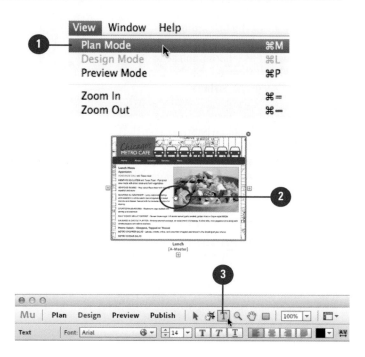

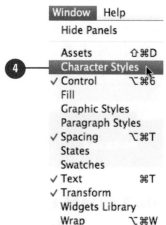

⑤ Click and drag over the text characters with the Text tool cursor.

⑥ Click the style name in the Character Styles panel.

Muse applies the saved character formatting attributes to the selected text object.

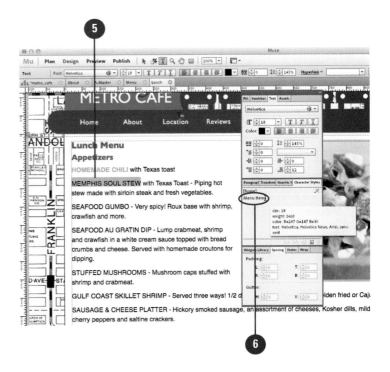

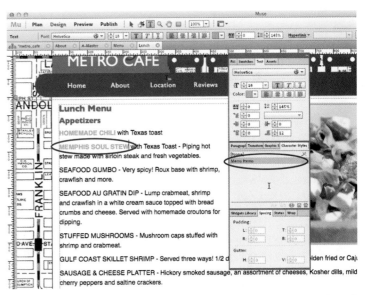

Muse applies the saved character formatting attributes to the selected text and highlights the style name in the Character Styles panel.

Applying a Paragraph Style

Applying paragraph styles in Muse is essentially the same as applying character styles. After you save your favorite attributes as a style, you can apply them to a selected text object by clicking the style name in the Paragraph Styles panel. Any additional attributes that you apply to a text object after applying the style are considered overrides. You can clear style overrides by Option-(Mac) or Alt-(Win) clicking the style name in the Paragraph Styles panel or by clicking the Clear Overrides button located at the bottom of the panel.

Click the style name in the Paragraph Styles panel

① Choose **Plan Mode** from the **View** menu.

TIMESAVER Press Cmd+M (Mac) or Ctrl+M (Win) to apply the Plan Mode command quickly.

② From the sitemap, double-click the thumbnail of a page whose text objects you'd like to apply a paragraph style to.

Muse opens the page in Design Mode.

③ Click the **Text Tool** icon at the top of the Design Mode interface.

TIMESAVER Press T to access the Text tool quickly.

④ To display the Paragraph Styles panel, choose **Window > Paragraph Styles**.

Did You Know?

The plus symbol means there is a style override. When you see a plus symbol (+) next to a style name in the Paragraph Styles panel, this indicates that additional attributes—that are not part of the style—have been applied to the object.

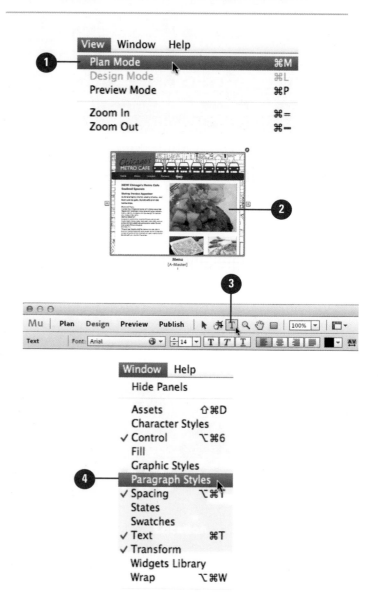

5 Insert the Text tool cursor anywhere in the paragraph you would like to stylize.

6 Click the style name in the Paragraph Styles panel.

Muse applies the saved formatting attributes to the selected text object.

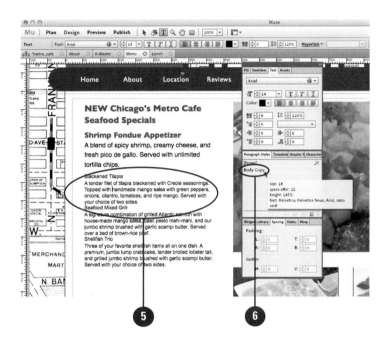

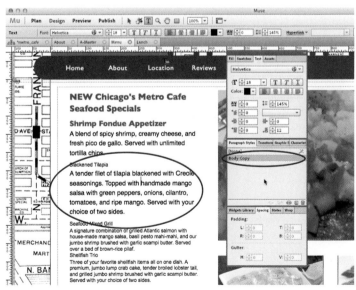

Muse applies the saved formatting attributes to the selected text and highlights the style name in the Paragraph Styles panel.

Applying Style Overrides

When you see a plus symbol (+) displayed next to a style name in the Character Styles or Paragraph Styles panel, this indicates that additional formatting attributes—that are not part of the applied style—have been added to the selected text object. You can apply style overrides by selecting a stylized text object and choosing different text formatting attributes from the Control panel or Text panel.

Add formatting to stylized text

1. Choose **Plan Mode** from the **View** menu.

   TIMESAVER *Press Cmd+M (Mac) or Ctrl+M (Win) to apply the Plan Mode command quickly.*

2. From the sitemap, double-click the thumbnail of a page whose text objects contain applied character or paragraph styles.

   Muse opens the page in Design Mode.

3. Click the **Text Tool** icon at the top of the Design Mode interface.

   TIMESAVER *Press T to access the Text tool quickly.*

4. To display the Character Styles or Paragraph Styles panel, choose **Window > Character Styles** or **Window > Paragraph Styles**.

5. Click and drag over the stylized text characters with the Text tool cursor.

6. In the Control panel or Text panel, choose the text formatting attributes that you would like to add to the stylized text.

   Muse displays a plus symbol (+) next to the style name in the Character Styles or Paragraph Styles panel to indicate that a style override has been applied.

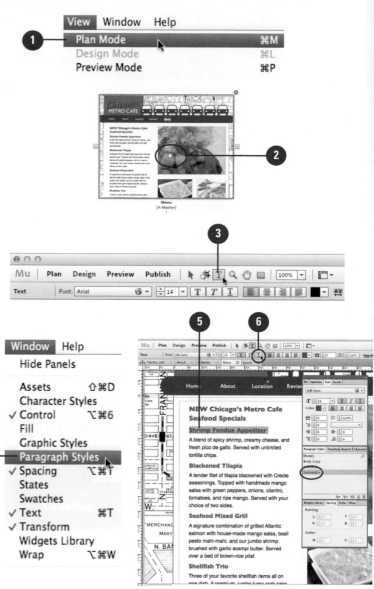

Muse displays a plus symbol (+) next to the style name.

Redefining Styles

Choose the Redefine Style command

① Choose **Plan Mode** from the **View** menu.

② From the sitemap, double-click the thumbnail of a page whose text objects contain style overrides.

Muse opens the page in Design Mode.

③ Click the **Text Tool** icon at the top of the Design Mode interface.

④ To display the Character Styles or Paragraph Styles panel, choose **Window > Character Styles** or **Window > Paragraph Styles**.

⑤ Insert the Text tool cursor anywhere in the paragraph (paragraph styles) or click and drag over the stylized text characters with the Text tool cursor (character styles).

⑥ Access the contextual menu by right-clicking or Control-clicking (Mac) the style name in the Character Styles or Paragraph Styles panel, and choose **Redefine Style**.

Muse redefines the style to include the formatting overrides.

Did You Know?

You can also redefine a style by clicking the Redefine Style button. To do so, select the object and click the Redefine Style button located at the bottom of the Character Styles or Paragraph Styles panel.

The only way to edit a character or paragraph style is to redefine it. You can add any applied overrides to the style definition by selecting the object and clicking the Redefine Style button located at the bottom of the Character Styles or Paragraph Styles panels. Alternatively, you can choose the Redefine Style command from the contextual menu by right-clicking or Control-clicking (Mac) the style name in its respective panel.

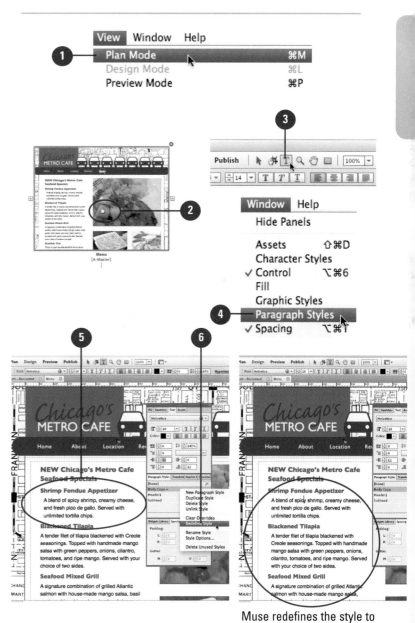

Muse redefines the style to include the formatting overrides.

Clearing Overrides

Choose the Clear Overrides command

1. Choose **Plan Mode** from the **View** menu.

2. From the sitemap, double-click the thumbnail of a page whose text objects contain style overrides.

   Muse opens the page in Design Mode.

3. Click the **Text Tool** icon at the top of the Design Mode interface.

4. To display the Character Styles or Paragraph Styles panel, choose **Window > Character Styles** or **Window > Paragraph Styles**.

5. Insert the Text tool cursor anywhere in the paragraph (paragraph styles) or click and drag over the stylized text characters with the Text tool cursor (character styles).

6. Access the contextual menu by right-clicking or Control-clicking (Mac) the style name in the Character Styles or Paragraph Styles panel, and choose **Clear Overrides**.

   Muse removes the additional formatting from the stylized text.

Did You Know?

You can also clear overrides by clicking the Clear Overrides button. To do so, select the object and click the Clear Overrides button located at the bottom of the Character Styles or Paragraph Styles panel.

Any additional attributes that you apply to a text object after applying a style are considered overrides. You can clear style overrides by Option-(Mac) or Alt-(Win) clicking the style name in the Character Styles or Paragraph Styles panel or by clicking the Clear Overrides button located at the bottom of either panel. You can also choose the Clear Overrides command from the contextual menu by right-clicking or Control-clicking (Mac) the style name.

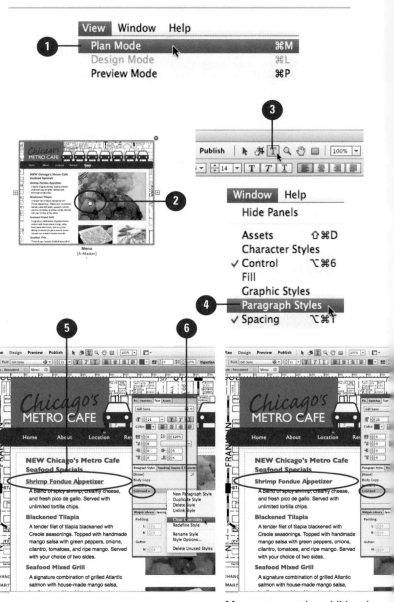

Muse removes the additional formatting from the stylized text.

Unlinking Styles

Choose the Unlink Style command

1 Choose **Plan Mode** from the **View** menu.

2 From the sitemap, double-click the thumbnail of a page whose text objects contain applied styles.

Muse opens the page in Design Mode.

3 Click the **Text Tool** icon at the top of the Design Mode interface.

4 To display the Character Styles or Paragraph Styles panel, choose **Window > Character Styles** or **Window > Paragraph Styles**.

5 Insert the Text tool cursor anywhere in the paragraph (paragraph styles) or click and drag over the stylized text characters with the Text tool cursor (character styles).

6 Access the contextual menu by right-clicking or Control-clicking (Mac) the style name in the Character Styles or Paragraph Styles panel, and choose **Unlink Style**.

Muse removes the style and maintains the text formatting.

Did You Know?

You can also unlink styles by clicking the Unlink Style button. To do so, select the object and click the Unlink Style button located at the bottom of the Character Styles or Paragraph Styles panel.

Unlinking styles removes a character or paragraph style while maintaining the applied text formatting. When you have a stylized text object selected in a layout, Muse highlights the name of the applied style in the Character Styles or Paragraph Styles panel. To unlink the object from the style, click the Unlink style button located at the bottom of either panel. You can also choose the Unlink style command from the contextual menu by right-clicking or Control-clicking (Mac) the style name.

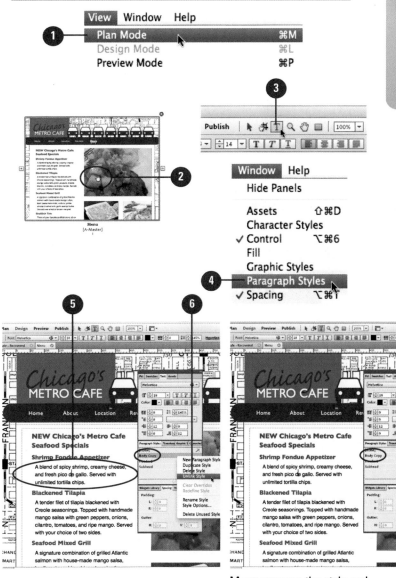

Muse removes the style and maintains the text formatting.

Deleting Styles

To delete a style from the Character Styles or Paragraph Styles panel, hover the cursor over the style name in the panel and right-click or Control-click (Mac) to access the contextual menu. Choose Delete Style to remove the style from the panel. If the style you are deleting is currently applied to any text objects in the site, Muse asks you what style you would like to use to replace it.

Choose the Delete Style command

1. Choose **Design Mode** from the **View** menu.

   TIMESAVER *Press Cmd+L (Mac) or Ctrl+L (Win) to apply the Design Mode command quickly.*

   Muse opens the current page in Design Mode.

2. To display the Character Styles or Paragraph Styles panel, choose **Window > Character Styles** or **Window > Paragraph Styles**.

3. Access the contextual menu by right-clicking or Control-clicking (Mac) the style name in the Character Styles or Paragraph Styles panel, and choose **Delete Style**.

   If the style is being used anywhere in the site, Muse displays the Replace Style window.

4. Select a style from the Replace Style list.

5. Click **Replace**.

   Any text objects that were stylized by the now deleted style assume the attributes of the replacement style.

   IMPORTANT *To replace a style with no style, choose None from the Replace Style list.*

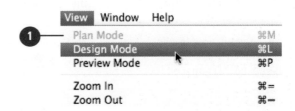

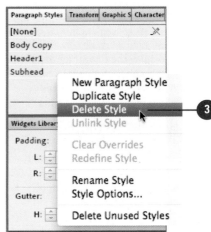

Applying Style Option Tags

In the Style Options dialog box, you can choose a different span tag to apply to a specific character style, or a different paragraph tag to apply to a paragraph style. Certain span tags, such as (em) for Emphasis, can help with search engine optimization when you export the site. Paragraph tags enable you to specify hierarchical HTML headers to use at site export, such as (h1) for top level headers, (h2) for subheads, and (p) for body copy.

Choose a span tag

1. Choose **Design Mode** from the **View** menu.

   TIMESAVER *Press Cmd+L (Mac) or Ctrl+L (Win) to apply the Design Mode command quickly.*

   Muse opens the current page in Design Mode.

2. To display the Character Styles panel, choose **Window > Character Styles**.

3. Access the contextual menu by right-clicking or Control-clicking (Mac) the style name in the Character Styles panel and choose **Style Options**.

   Muse displays the Style Options dialog box.

4. Choose a new span tag from the **Span Tag** drop-down list.

5. Click **OK** to close the Style Options dialog box.

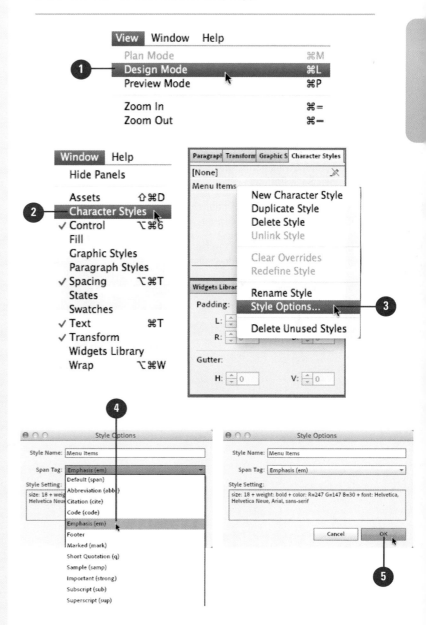

Choose a paragraph tag

① Choose **Design Mode** from the **View** menu.

TIMESAVER *Press Cmd+L (Mac) or Ctrl+L (Win) to apply the Design Mode command quickly.*

Muse opens the current page in Design Mode.

② To display the Paragraph Styles panel, choose **Window > Paragraph Styles**.

③ Access the contextual menu by right-clicking or Control-clicking (Mac) the style name in the Paragraph Styles panel and choose **Style Options**.

Muse displays the Style Options dialog box.

④ Choose a new paragraph tag from the **Paragraph Tag** drop-down list.

⑤ Click **OK** to close the Style Options dialog box.

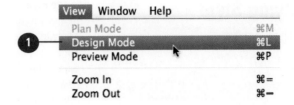

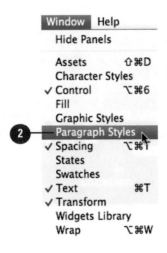

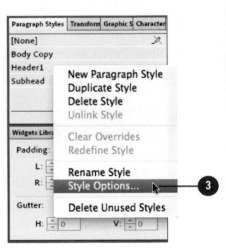

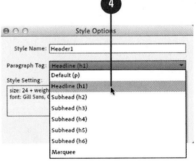

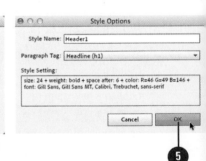

Adding Hyperlinks

9

Introduction

Hyperlinks are essential to any website. Just think. Without them, you would be stuck forever on the same page! Thankfully, creating hyperlinks in Muse is incredibly easy.

When you utilize the prebuilt, editable menu widgets in Muse, the page links are automatically generated for you (see Chapter 4, "Adding Navigational Content"). However, along with these auto-generated page links, you can apply additional hyperlinks to selected text and graphic objects throughout your site.

In this chapter, you'll learn how to create hyperlinks that take you to another page in your site, as well as how to create links that take you to an entirely different website. This chapter also explains how to create email links.

You'll also learn to create and apply link styles to editable text links. These link styles enable you to control the link's appearance (color, bold, italic, and underline) during its different states (Normal, Hover, Visited, Active).

In the last sections of this chapter, you'll learn to use the Link Anchor place cursor to assign anchored links to your pages.

What You'll Do

Creating a Link to a Page Within the Site

Creating an External URL Link

Inserting an Email Link

Previewing a Hyperlink

Creating a Link Style

Applying Link Styles

Inserting a Link Anchor

Applying a Hyperlink to an Anchor

Creating a Link to a Page Within the Site

Choose a page from the Hyperlink list

1 Choose **Plan Mode** from the **View** menu.

> **TIMESAVER** *Press Cmd+M (Mac) or Ctrl+M (Win) to apply the Plan Mode command quickly.*

2 From the sitemap, double-click the thumbnail of the page you'd like to add a hyperlink to.

Muse opens the page in Design Mode.

3 Click the **Text Tool** icon at the top of the Design Mode interface.

> **TIMESAVER** *Press T to access the Text Tool quickly.*

4 Using the Text tool cursor, click and drag over the text characters you would like to add a hyperlink to.

Muse highlights the characters as you drag to let you know they are now selected.

5 Choose the page to which you want to link from the Hyperlink drop-down list.

Muse generates the hyperlink using the default link style.

Did You Know?

You can also apply page links to graphics. To do so, select the graphic with the Selection tool and choose the page from the Hyperlink drop-down list.

Muse automatically generates the page links for you when you utilize the prebuilt menus available in the Widgets Library panel (see Chapter 4, "Adding Navigational Content"). However, you can create additional hyperlinks that take you to the other pages in your site by selecting the text or object and choosing the page from the Hyperlink drop-down list, which is accessible via the Control panel.

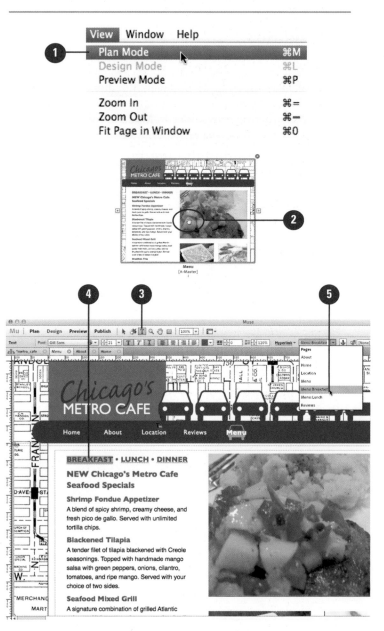

Creating an External URL Link

Enter the website URL in the Hyperlink field

① Choose **Plan Mode** from the **View** menu.

> **TIMESAVER** *Press Cmd+M (Mac) or Ctrl+M (Win) to apply the Plan Mode command quickly.*

② From the sitemap, double-click the thumbnail of the page you'd like to add a hyperlink to.

Muse opens the page in Design Mode.

③ Click the **Text Tool** icon at the top of the Design Mode interface.

> **TIMESAVER** *Press T to access the Text tool quickly.*

④ Using the Text tool cursor, click and drag over the text characters you would like to add a hyperlink to.

Muse highlights the characters as you drag to let you know they are now selected.

⑤ Enter the full website URL in the Hyperlink field of the Control panel.

Muse generates the hyperlink using the Default Link Style.

Did You Know?

You can also apply external links to graphics. To do so, select the graphic with the Selection tool and enter the full website URL in the Hyperlink field.

In addition to internal page links, you can create links that take you to an external website. To do so, select the text or object and enter the full website URL (including "http://") in the Control panel Hyperlink field. By default, Muse always applies the Default Link Style to external text links, but you can apply other link styles via the Text Link Style drop-down list in the Hyperlinks drop-down window (see "Applying Link Styles" later in this chapter).

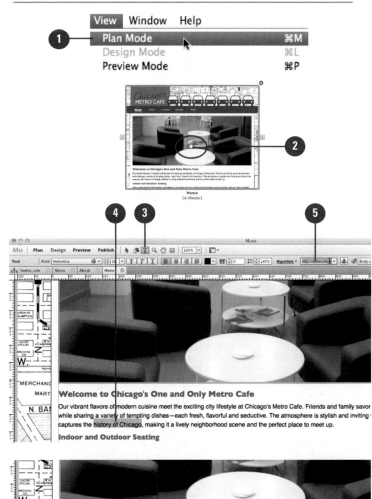

Muse generates the hyperlink using the Default Link Style.

Inserting an Email Link

You can also create email links in Muse. To do so, select the text you'd like to apply the email link to and enter the full email, preceded by "mailto:" (without quotes) in the Control panel Hyperlink field. When you click the email link in Preview Mode to test it, Muse should open a new, blank message in your default email application, with the email address already entered in the To field.

Enter the email in the Hyperlink field

① Choose **Plan Mode** from the **View** menu.

> **TIMESAVER** *Press Cmd+M (Mac) or Ctrl+M (Win) to apply the Plan Mode command quickly.*

② From the sitemap, double-click the thumbnail of the page you'd like to add an email link to.

> Muse opens the page in Design Mode.

③ Click the **Text Tool** icon at the top of the Design Mode interface.

> **TIMESAVER** *Press T to access the Text tool quickly.*

④ Using the Text tool cursor, click and drag over the text characters you would like to add an email link to.

> Muse highlights the characters as you drag to let you know they are now selected.

⑤ In the Hyperlink field of the Control panel, enter "mailto:" (without quotes) followed by the email address.

> Muse generates the email link using the Default Link Style.

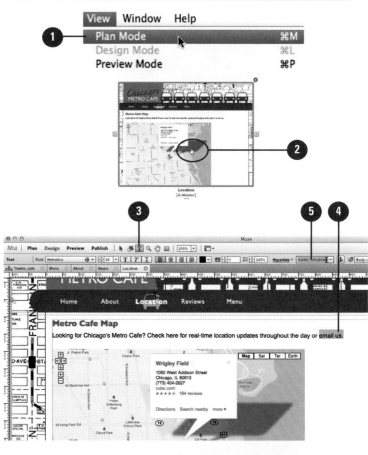

Muse generates the hyperlink using the default link style.

Previewing a Hyperlink

After you create a hyperlink, you should always test it in Preview Mode to make sure it is functioning properly. You also want to make sure that the link's appearance in each of its states (Normal, Hover, Visited, and Active) is the way you would like it. If not, you can always create or apply a different link style in Design Mode (see "Creating a Link Style" and "Applying Link Styles" later in this chapter).

Choose the Preview command

1. Choose **Plan Mode** from the **View** menu.

   TIMESAVER *Press Cmd+M (Mac) or Ctrl+M (Win) to apply the Plan Mode command quickly.*

2. From the sitemap, double-click the thumbnail of the page whose link you'd like to preview.

   Muse opens the page in Design Mode.

3. Choose **View > Preview Mode** or click the **Preview** button located in the upper left of the Design Mode interface.

   TIMESAVER *Press Cmd+P (Mac) or Ctrl+P (Win) to apply the Preview Mode command quickly.*

4. Hover the cursor over the hyperlink and click to test it.

Did You Know?

You can force a link to open in a separate window or tab. To do so, click the Hyperlink button in the Control panel to display the Hyperlink drop-down window. Proceed to enable the Open Link in New Window or Tab option available in the window.

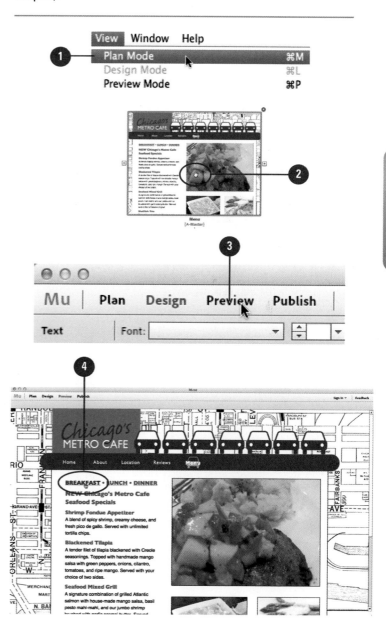

Creating a Link Style

By default, Muse applies the Default Link Style to every text link you create. In most cases, the Default Link Style appearance attributes are not going to match your site design. Thankfully, you can edit the Default Link Style and create your own link styles. The Hyperlinks controls in the Site Properties dialog box enable you to choose the appearance attributes (color, bold, italic, and underline) for each state of the link (Normal, Hover, Visited, and Active).

Choose Edit Link Styles

① From any View Mode, choose **File > Site Properties.**

Muse displays the Site Properties dialog box.

② Click the **Hyperlinks** button at the top of the Site Properties dialog box.

Muse displays the Link Style Options in the Site Properties dialog box.

③ Click the **New Link Style** button in the Site Properties dialog box.

By default, Muse names the new link style **[Default Link Style] copy**.

④ To rename the style, double-click **[Default Link Style] copy** from the Link Styles list.

Muse highlights the style name in the Character Styles panel.

Did You Know?

You can also access the Site Properties dialog box from the Control Panel. To do so, access the Hyperlink drop-down window by clicking the Hyperlink button in the Control panel. To access the Site Properties dialog box, click the Edit Link Styles button in the drop-down window.

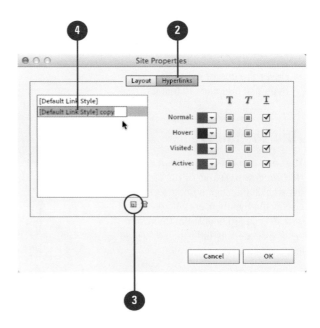

⑤ Enter a name for the style and press Return (Mac) or Enter (Win).

⑥ Choose a color for each hyperlink state (Normal, Hover, Visited, and Active) by clicking the **Color Swatch** icon next to each one.

Muse displays the Color Picker.

⑦ Using the Color Picker, choose a color for the link state using any of the following methods:

◆ Enter values into the **RGB** fields.

◆ Enter a hexadecimal code in the **Hex#** field.

◆ Click a **swatch** from the saved **color swatch list**.

◆ Drag the **Hue** slider up or down to select a color hue. Then click in the color field to the right of the Hue slider to determine the saturation and brightness of the selected color.

◆ Click the **Sample Color tool** icon. To sample a color for the link state, proceed to click anywhere on the page—including in a placed photo or graphic.

Click away to apply the new text color.

Muse applies the new color to the link state.

⑧ For each link state, click the **Bold**, **Italic**, or **Underline** checkboxes to enable that text style.

⑨ Click **OK** to close the Site Properties dialog box.

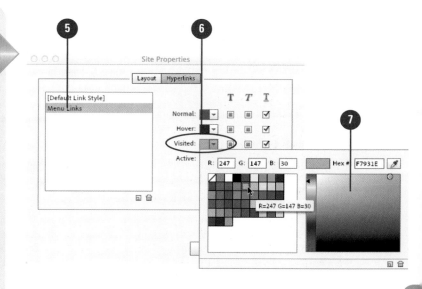

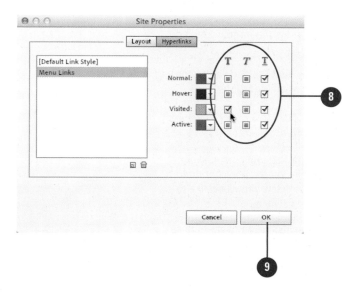

Applying Link Styles

You can apply different text link styles at any time by selecting the text link in your layout and choosing a different style from the Text Link Style list. To access the Text Link Style list, you must display the Hyperlinks drop-down window by clicking the Hyperlink button in the Control panel. As you click the style name in the list, Muse applies it to the selected text link in the layout.

Choose the link style from the Site Properties dialog box

1 Choose **Plan Mode** from the **View** menu.

> **TIMESAVER** *Press Cmd+M (Mac) or Ctrl+M (Win) to apply the Plan Mode command quickly.*

2 From the sitemap, double-click the thumbnail of the page whose links you'd like to apply a link style to.

Muse opens the page in Design Mode.

3 Click the **Text Tool** icon at the top of the Design Mode interface.

> **TIMESAVER** *Press T to access the Text tool quickly.*

4 Using the Text tool cursor, click and drag over the text characters of the hyperlink you would like to add a link style to.

Muse highlights the characters as you drag to let you know they are now selected.

5 Click the **Hyperlink** button in the Control panel.

Muse displays the Hyperlink drop-down window.

6 In the Hyperlink drop-down window, choose the link style from the Text Link Style drop-down list.

Muse applies the link style to the selected hyperlink.

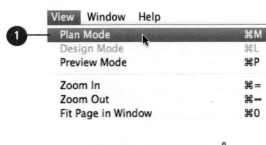

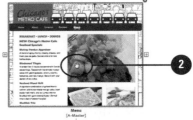

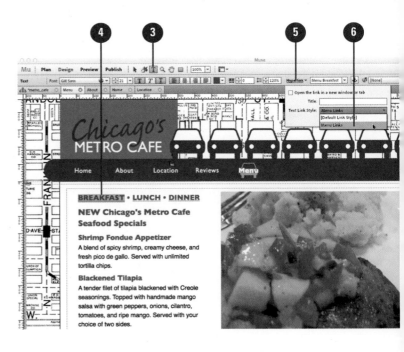

7 Choose **View > Preview Mode** or click the **Preview** button located in the upper left of the Design Mode interface.

TIMESAVER *Press Cmd+P (Mac) or Ctrl+P (Win) to apply the Preview Mode command quickly.*

8 Hover the cursor over the hyperlink and click to test it.

Did You Know?

Link styles are treated as paragraph attributes. As a result, if you create a paragraph style based on a paragraph with a link style applied, Muse automatically includes the link style in the paragraph style. This means that all links in a single paragraph must use the same link style in order to create a paragraph style from it.

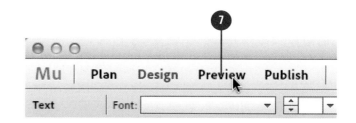

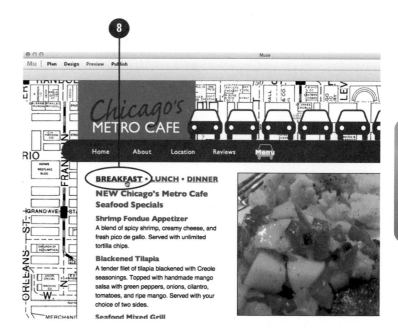

Inserting a Link Anchor

Another type of link you can create in Muse is an anchored link. These types of links can take you to a specific location on the active page or to a specific location on another page within the site. To create an anchored link, you must click the Link Anchor button in the Control panel. Doing so loads the Link Anchor place tool cursor. Click anywhere on the page with the place tool to create a link anchor.

Click the Link Anchor button

1. Choose **Plan Mode** from the **View** menu.

   TIMESAVER Press Cmd+M (Mac) or Ctrl+M (Win) to apply the Plan Mode command quickly.

2. From the sitemap, double-click the thumbnail of the page you'd like to apply a link anchor to.

   Muse opens the page in Design Mode.

3. Click the **Link Anchor** button in the Control panel.

   TIMESAVER Press A to load the Link Anchor place tool quickly.

4. To place the anchor, click the loaded **Link Anchor** place tool anywhere on the page (or a separate, open page).

   Muse opens the Create an Anchor dialog box.

5. Enter a name for the anchor in the Create an Anchor dialog box.

6. Click **OK** to close the Create an Anchor dialog box.

   Muse displays a link anchor icon wherever you clicked with the **Link Anchor** place tool.

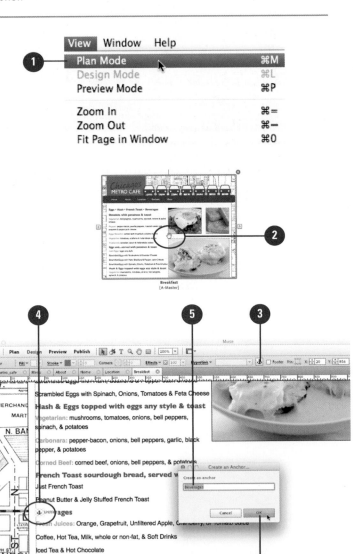

Applying a Hyperlink to an Anchor

After you insert a link anchor on a page, Muse adds the link name to the Hyperlink drop-down list in the Control panel. You can then apply the anchor link to any selected text, just as you would when creating a hyperlink (see "Creating a Page Link" earler in this chapter). Anchor links always appear at the bottom of the Hyperlink drop-down list. Anchor links that take you to a specific location on the active page utilize smooth scrolling in a browser.

Choose the link anchor from the Hyperlink drop-down list

1. Choose **Plan Mode** from the **View** menu.

    TIMESAVER *Press Cmd+M (Mac) or Ctrl+M (Win) to apply the Plan Mode command quickly.*

2. From the sitemap, double-click the thumbnail of the page you'd like to apply a link anchor to.

    Muse opens the page in Design Mode.

3. Click the **Text Tool** icon at the top of the Design Mode interface.

    TIMESAVER *Press T to access the Text tool quickly.*

4. Using the Text tool cursor, click and drag over the text characters you would like to add a hyperlink to.

    Muse highlights the characters as you drag to let you know they are now selected.

5. In the Control panel, choose the anchor link from the Hyperlink drop-down list.

    Muse generates the hyperlink using the Default Link Style.

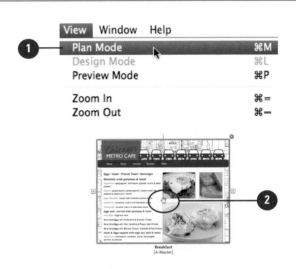

6 Choose **View > Preview Mode** or click the **Preview** button located in the upper left of the Design Mode interface.

TIMESAVER *Press Cmd+P (Mac) or Ctrl+P (Win) to apply the Preview Mode command quickly.*

7 Hover the cursor over the hyperlink, and click to test it.

Did You Know?

You can also apply anchor links to graphics. To do so, select the graphic with the Selection tool. Then in the Control panel, choose the anchor link from the Hyperlink drop-down list.

Did You Know?

You can show and hide link anchors in Design Mode. To show and hide link anchors from the page, choose Show/Hide Link Anchors from the View menu.

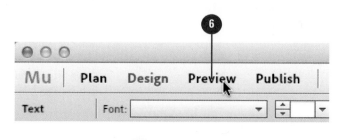

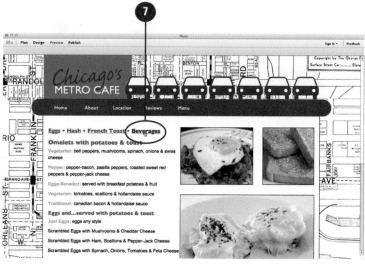

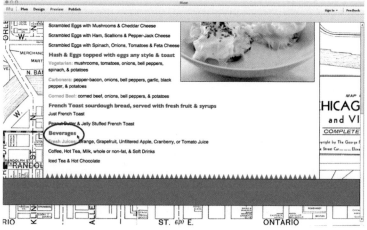

Anchor links utilize smooth scrolling in Preview Mode.

Working with Slideshows and Compositions

10

Introduction

Slideshows are great for showcasing photographs at online portfolio sites, but they're also commonly used at news sites and online stores. You might think that setting up slideshows like these would be difficult, but it's actually very easy when you use the slideshow and composition widgets available in Muse.

The prebuilt slideshow and composition widgets are available via the Widgets Library panel. You can add one by dragging it from the Widgets Library panel onto the page. In this chapter, you will learn how to customize the prebuilt slideshow widgets to better suit the overall design of your site.

You will learn how to add and delete slideshow images, as well as how to resize and reposition the hero images and image thumbnails. In addition, you will learn how to edit and reformat slideshow text objects and apply rollover functionality to slideshow thumbnails.

The final sections of the chapter explain how to choose slideshow options, such as those for transition and auto-play. They also explain how to enable or disable the light-box feature and show or hide various slideshow parts, such as the slide counter, close button, or caption.

Adding a Slideshow or Composition

Slideshows are commonly used in online portfolios to show examples of an artist's work. You'll also find slideshows at many popular news sites to display the latest headlines. Slideshows are even used at online shopping sites to display photos of a product taken from different angles. Thankfully, Muse makes adding slideshows to your sites incredibly easy via widgets and the Widgets Library panel. To add a prebuilt slideshow or composition widget, all you need to do is click and drag the item from the Widgets Library onto the page. You can then customize the slideshow to suit your website's design by resizing, repositioning, and editing the widget contents.

Drag-and-drop the Slideshow or Composition widget

1. Choose **Plan Mode** from the **View** menu.

   TIMESAVER *Press Cmd+M (Mac) or Ctrl+M (Win) to apply the Plan Mode command quickly.*

2. From the sitemap, double-click the thumbnail of the page you'd like to add a slideshow to.

   Muse opens the page in Design Mode.

3. If it's not visible already, choose **Window > Widgets Library** to display the Widgets Library panel.

4. Click the right-facing arrow next to **Compositions** or **Slideshows** in the **Widgets Library** panel.

   Muse displays the available widget options, including **Blank**, **Featured News**, **Lightbox Display**, **Presentation**, and **Tooltip** (Compositions); and **Basic**, **Blank**, **Lightbox**, and **Thumbnails** (Slideshows).

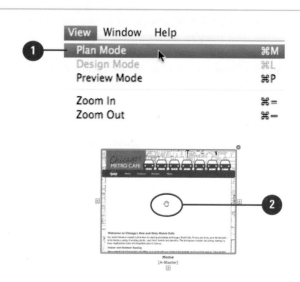

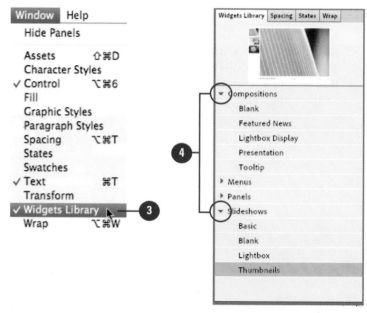

5 Click and drag the Slideshow
widget from the **Widgets Library**
panel onto the page.

5

Did You Know?

***The Widgets Library panel also
includes menus and panels.*** You can
also drag prebuilt menu and panel
widgets from the Widgets Library panel
onto a page (see Chapter 4 "Adding
Navigational Content").

Placing Photos in a Slideshow

The prebuilt slideshow and composition widgets in Muse come equipped with placeholder photographs. You can easily remove these photos and include photos of your own. To do so, choose the Place command, or click the Add Images button in the slideshow Options panel. By default, when you add slideshow images, Muse crops the hero and thumbnail images differently. Hero images fit the frame proportionally (leaving white space in the frame), while thumbnail images fill the frame proportionally (cropping the image to fill the frame). You can change these frame options in the slideshow Options flyout window, accessible by clicking the blue arrow to the right of the widget.

Choose the Place command

1. Choose **Plan Mode** from the **View** menu.

    TIMESAVER *Press Cmd+M (Mac) or Ctrl+M (Win) to apply the Plan Mode command quickly.*

2. From the sitemap, double-click the thumbnail of the page whose slideshow you'd like to edit.

    Muse opens the page in Design Mode.

3. Choose **File > Place** to access the Import dialog box.

4. Using the Import dialog box, navigate to the slideshow images on your system disk. Shift-click to select multiple consecutive images; Cmd-click (Mac) or Ctrl-click (Win) to select multiple non-consecutive images.

    IMPORTANT *You can only import images saved in the following file formats: PNG, PSD, JPEG, and GIF.*

5. Click **Select** to close the Import dialog box and import the images.

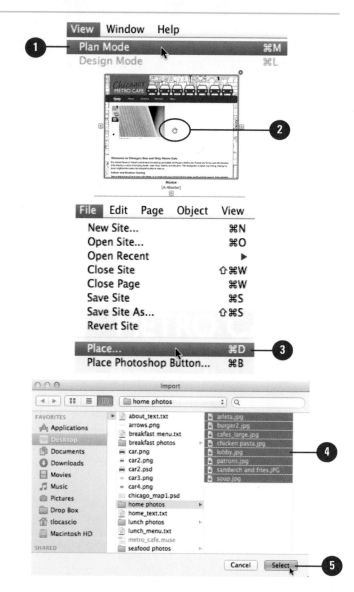

6 To place the images, click the loaded place cursor on the slideshow widget.

By default, Muse automatically sizes the images to fill the slideshow thumbnail frames and fit the hero frame.

Muse places the images in the slideshow automatically.

Click the Add Images button

1. Choose **Plan Mode** from the **View** menu.

2. From the sitemap, double-click the thumbnail of the page whose slideshow you'd like to edit.

   Muse opens the page in Design Mode.

3. Click the **Selection Tool** icon at the top of the Design Mode interface.

4. Click anywhere on the slideshow widget to select it.

5. Click the right-facing arrow that appears in the upper-right corner of the selected slideshow widget.

   Muse displays a flyout Options panel.

6. In the flyout Options panel, click the **Add Images** button.

   Muse displays the Import dialog box.

7. Using the Import dialog box, navigate to the slideshow images on your system disk. Shift-click to select multiple consecutive images; Cmd-click (Mac) or Ctrl-click (Win) to select multiple non-consecutive images.

   IMPORTANT *You can only import images saved in the following file formats: PNG, PSD, JPEG, and GIF.*

8. Click Select to close the Import dialog box and place the new images in the slideshow.

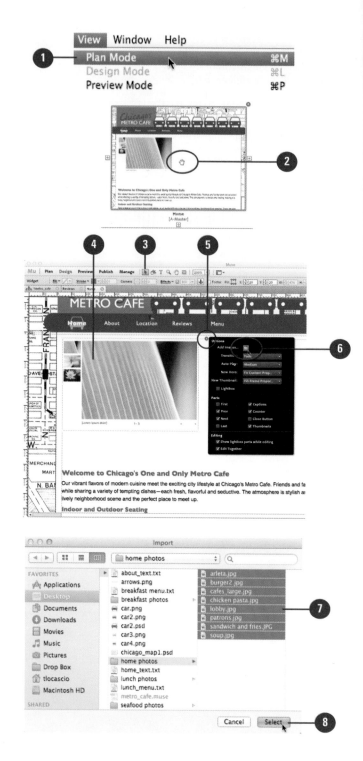

By default, Muse automatically sizes the images to fill the slideshow thumbnail frames and fit the hero frame.

Muse places the images in the slideshow automatically.

Removing Photos from a Slideshow

One of the first things you'll want to do when creating a slideshow is to delete the placeholder photographs that are part of the slideshow or composition widget. As you customize your slideshow, you may also decide to remove some images of your own. To delete a photo from a slideshow or composition, select the image thumbnail or hero image with the Selection tool and press Delete or Backspace (Win). Doing so removes both the thumbnail image and its frame container.

Delete the selected slideshow image thumbnail

① Choose **Plan Mode** from the **View** menu.

TIMESAVER *Press Cmd+M (Mac) or Ctrl+M (Win) to apply the Plan Mode command quickly.*

② From the sitemap, double-click the thumbnail of the page whose slideshow you'd like to edit.

Muse opens the page in Design Mode.

③ Click the **Selection Tool** icon at the top of the Design Mode interface.

TIMESAVER *Press V to access the Selection tool quickly.*

④ To select the image you'd like to remove from the slideshow, click its thumbnail three times, or click the hero image twice.

⑤ Press **Delete** or **Backspace** (Win).

Muse removes the image from the slideshow.

Did You Know?

You can also add object formatting to slideshow images. To do so, select the slideshow image with the Selection tool and choose the object attributes, such as stroke, effects, and opacity from the Control panel.

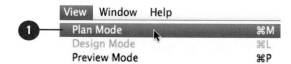

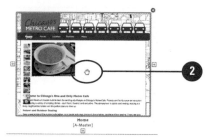

Resizing Slideshow Images

One of the great things about working with slideshow and composition widgets is that you can easily customize them to better suit your website design. For example, you may want to resize the hero image to be bigger and the thumbnails to be smaller, or vice versa. Resizing slideshow image frames is no different from resizing any other frame in Muse. To resize both the image and its frame container proportionally, click and drag any corner selection node.

Drag a side or corner node with the Selection tool

1. Choose **Plan Mode** from the **View** menu.

   TIMESAVER *Press Cmd+M (Mac) or Ctrl+M (Win) to apply the Plan Mode command quickly.*

2. From the sitemap, double-click the thumbnail of the page whose slideshow you'd like to edit.

   Muse opens the page in Design Mode.

3. Click the **Selection Tool** icon at the top of the Design Mode interface.

   TIMESAVER *Press V to access the Selection tool quickly.*

4. To select the slideshow image you'd like to resize, click its thumbnail three times, or click the hero image twice.

5. Click and drag any corner or side node to resize the selected slideshow image.

   IMPORTANT *As you resize the image, Muse displays the current scale percentage next to the Selection tool cursor.*

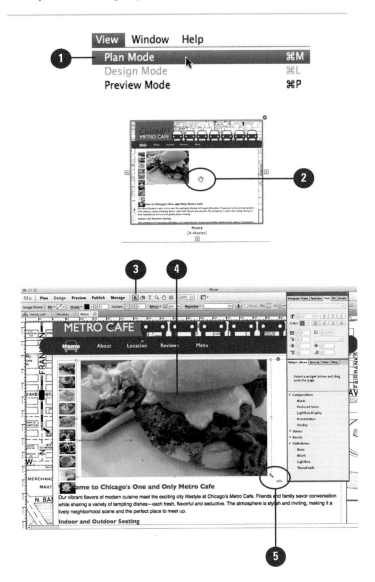

Repositioning Slideshow Elements

All widget slideshow elements, such as the image thumbnails, the hero image, the caption, the previous and next buttons, and any additional parts you've made visible from the slideshow Options window, can be selected and repositioned. By default, these slideshow elements are all grouped together; however, Muse enables you to select each one from within the group and move it to a new location on the page. When you deselect the repositioned object, it still remains in the group.

Click and drag slideshow elements

1. Choose **Plan Mode** from the **View** menu.

   TIMESAVER *Press Cmd+M (Mac) or Ctrl+M (Win) to apply the Plan Mode command quickly.*

2. From the sitemap, double-click the thumbnail of the page whose slideshow you'd like to edit.

   Muse opens the page in Design Mode.

3. Click the **Selection Tool** icon at the top of the Design Mode interface.

   TIMESAVER *Press V to access the Selection tool quickly.*

4. To select the slideshow object you would like to reposition, click it with the **Selection** tool.

   IMPORTANT *Depending on which slideshow object you are trying to select, you may have to click two or three times with the Selection tool.*

5. Click and drag to reposition the slideshow object.

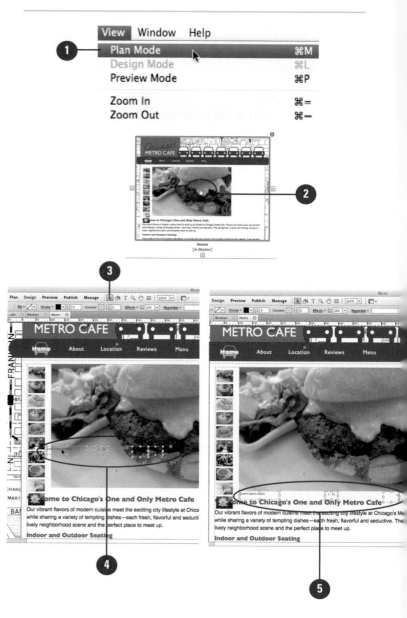

156

Editing Slideshow Text

The sample text that appears in captions for widget slideshows and compositions is also entirely editable. You can enter new text, resize and reposition text frames, and apply different text formatting or styles. Note that as you edit related slideshow text objects, such as the Prev and Next buttons, the changes are automatically applied globally. This is because the Edit Together option is enabled by default in the slideshow Options window, accessible by clicking the blue arrow to the right of the widget.

Edit slideshow text and formatting

1. Choose **Plan Mode** from the **View** menu.

   TIMESAVER *Press Cmd+M (Mac) or Ctrl+M (Win) to apply the Plan Mode command quickly.*

2. From the sitemap, double-click the thumbnail of the page whose slideshow you'd like to edit.

   Muse opens the page in Design Mode.

3. Click the **Text Tool** icon at the top of the Design Mode interface.

   TIMESAVER *Press T to access the Text tool quickly.*

4. To select the text you would like to edit, click and drag over the characters with the Text tool cursor.

5. Enter new formatting attributes in the Control panel or Text panel.

6. Enter new text for the caption.

> ### See Also
> *See Chapter 7, "Working with Text," to learn more about applying text attributes.*

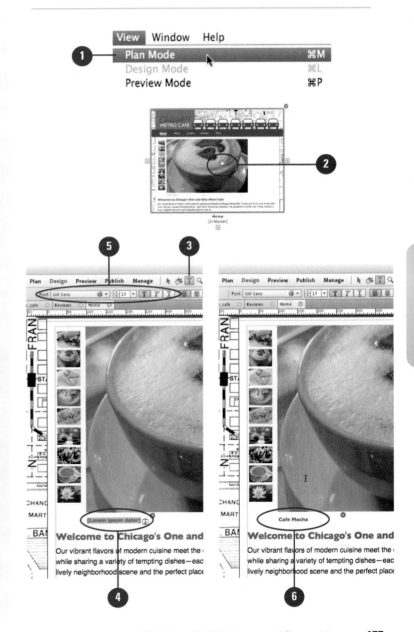

Working with Slideshows and Compositions **157**

Editing Slideshow Thumbnail States

Slideshow thumbnails can also include rollover functionality. You can edit rollover states for a thumbnail by selecting it and clicking one of the four states from the States panel (Normal, Rollover, Mouse Down, and Active). You can then choose specific appearance attributes for each state from the Control panel. Note that as you apply edits to a thumbnail state, the changes are automatically applied to all of the thumbnails in the slideshow. This is because the Edit Together option is enabled by default in the slideshow Options window, accessible by clicking the blue arrow to the right of the widget.

Edit rollover states with the States panel

1. Choose **Plan Mode** from the **View** menu.

   TIMESAVER *Press Cmd+M (Mac) or Ctrl+M (Win) to apply the Plan Mode command quickly.*

2. From the sitemap, double-click the thumbnail of the page whose slideshow you'd like to edit.

   Muse opens the page in Design Mode.

3. Click the **Selection Tool** icon at the top of the Design Mode interface.

   TIMESAVER *Press V to access the Selection tool quickly.*

4. Triple-click one of the slideshow thumbnails to select it.

5. Choose **Window > States** to display the **States** panel.

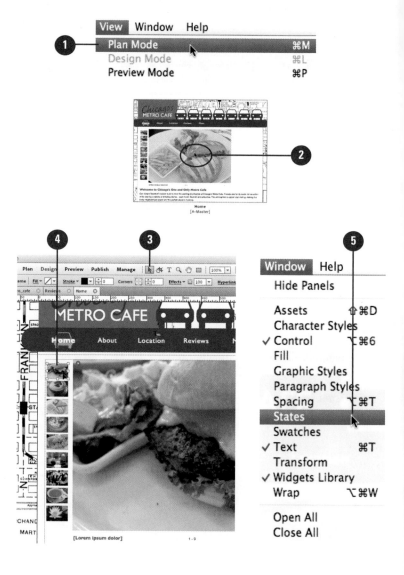

6 Click the **Normal** state in the States panel.

7 From the **Control** panel, choose the preferred normal state attributes, such as Opacity, Stroke, and Effects.

8 Click the **Rollover** state in the States panel.

9 From the **Control** panel, choose the preferred rollover state attributes, such as Opacity, Stroke, and Effects.

10 Click the **Mouse Down** state in the States panel.

11 From the **Control** panel, choose the preferred mouse down state attributes, such as Opacity, Stroke, and Effects.

12 Click the **Active** state in the States panel.

13 From the **Control** panel, choose the preferred active state attributes, such as Opacity, Stroke, and Effects.

Muse updates the different thumbnail rollover states.

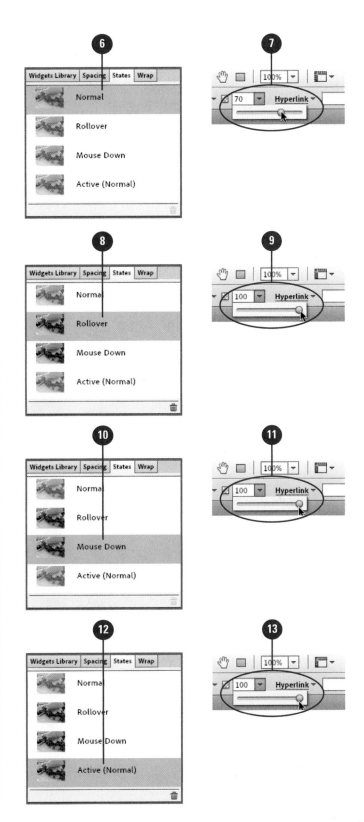

14 Choose **View > Preview Mode** or click the **Preview** button located in the upper left of the Design Mode interface.

Muse opens the page in Preview Mode, where you can preview the new thumbnail rollover states.

Muse opens the page in Preview Mode.

Choosing Slideshow Transition Options

Muse also enables you to control the way the images transition from one to another when playing the slideshow. By clicking the right-facing arrow that appears in the upper-right corner of a slideshow, you can access the Options flyout window. Here you can choose a transition option from the Transition list. Options include Fade (the default option), Horizontal, and Vertical.

Choose a transition option from the Transition list

1. Choose **Plan Mode** from the **View** menu.

2. From the sitemap, double-click the thumbnail of the page whose slideshow you'd like to edit.

   Muse opens the page in Design Mode.

3. Click the **Selection Tool** icon at the top of the Design Mode interface.

4. Click anywhere on the slideshow widget to select it.

5. Click the right-facing arrow that appears in the upper-right corner of the selected slideshow widget.

   Muse displays a flyout Options panel.

6. In the flyout Options panel, choose a transition option from the **Transition** list. Options include **Fade, Horizontal,** and **Vertical**.

7. Choose **View > Preview Mode** or click the **Preview** button located in the upper left of the Design Mode interface.

   TIMESAVER *Press Cmd+P (Mac) or Ctrl+P (Win) to apply the Preview Mode command quickly.*

   Muse opens the page in Preview Mode, where you can preview the new slideshow transitions.

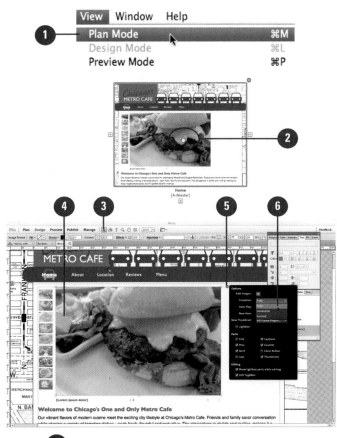

Choosing Slideshow Autoplay Options

You can control the speed at which each image displays in the slideshow by choosing an Auto Play option. To access these options, you must display the Options flyout window. You can do so by clicking the right-facing arrow in the upper-right corner of a selected slideshow. From the Auto Play list in the Options window, you can choose None, Slow, Medium (the default), or Fast.

Choose an Auto Play option from the Auto Play list

1. Choose **Plan Mode** from the **View** menu.

2. From the sitemap, double-click the thumbnail of the page whose slideshow you'd like to edit.

   Muse opens the page in Design Mode.

3. Click the **Selection Tool** icon at the top of the Design Mode interface.

4. Click anywhere on the slideshow widget to select it.

5. Click the right-facing arrow that appears in the upper-right corner of the selected slideshow widget.

   Muse displays a flyout Options panel.

6. In the flyout Options panel, choose a transition option from the **Auto Play** list. Options include **None**, **Slow**, **Medium**, and **Fast**.

7. Choose **View > Preview Mode** or click the **Preview** button located in the upper left of the Design Mode interface.

   TIMESAVER *Press Cmd+P (Mac) or Ctrl+P (Win) to apply the Preview Mode command quickly.*

   Muse opens the page in Preview Mode, where you can preview the new auto play options.

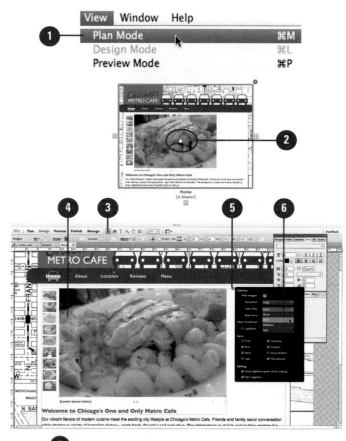

Enabling the Lightbox Option

When you enable the Lightbox feature in Muse, the slideshow behaves differently during playback. With Lightbox enabled, the entire web page is dimmed during playback, except for the slideshow hero. This puts extra emphasis on the images you are showcasing. You can enable the Lightbox feature from within the slideshow Options window.

Enable the Lightbox option in the Slideshow Options window

① Choose **Plan Mode** from the **View** menu.

TIMESAVER *Press Cmd+M (Mac) or Ctrl+M (Win) to apply the Plan Mode command quickly.*

② From the sitemap, double-click the thumbnail of the page whose slideshow you'd like to edit.

Muse opens the page in Design Mode.

③ Click the **Selection Tool** icon at the top of the Design Mode interface.

TIMESAVER *Press V to access the Selection tool quickly.*

④ Click anywhere on the slideshow widget to select it.

⑤ Click the right-facing arrow that appears in the upper-right corner of the selected slideshow widget.

Muse displays a flyout Options panel.

⑥ Enable the **Lightbox** option in the flyout Options panel.

IMPORTANT *Enabling the Lightbox option may require that you reposition or resize certain slideshow parts, such as captions, prev and next buttons, and the counter.*

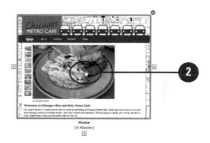

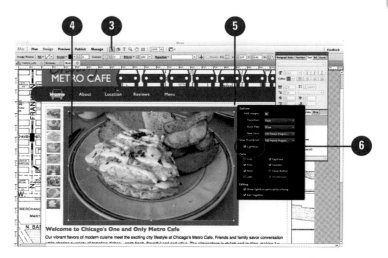

7 Choose **View > Preview Mode** or click the **Preview** button located in the upper left of the Design Mode interface.

TIMESAVER *Press Cmd+P (Mac) or Ctrl+P (Win) to apply the Preview Mode command quickly.*

Muse opens the page in Preview Mode, where you can test the functionality and appearance of the lightbox.

Muse opens the page in Preview Mode.

Enabling and Disabling Slideshow Parts

Different slideshow widgets display different items, such as thumbnails, previous and next buttons, captions, and a counter. You can control which items are displayed by placing a check next to each one in the Parts section of the Slideshow Options window. Other items you can include in your custom slideshows are first and last buttons and a close button.

Choose a transition option from the Transition list

1. Choose **Plan Mode** from the **View** menu.

2. From the sitemap, double-click the thumbnail of the page whose slideshow you'd like to edit.

   Muse opens the page in Design Mode.

3. Click the **Selection Tool** icon at the top of the Design Mode interface.

4. Click anywhere on the slideshow widget to select it.

5. Click the right-facing arrow that appears in the upper-right corner of the selected slideshow widget.

   Muse displays a flyout Options panel.

6. In the **Parts** section of the flyout Options panel, place a check next to each item you would like to include in the slideshow.

7. Choose **View > Preview Mode** or click the **Preview** button located in the upper left of the Design Mode interface.

   TIMESAVER *Press Cmd+P (Mac) or Ctrl+P (Win) to apply the Preview Mode command quickly.*

   Muse opens the page in Preview Mode, where you can test the functionality and appearance of the slideshow parts.

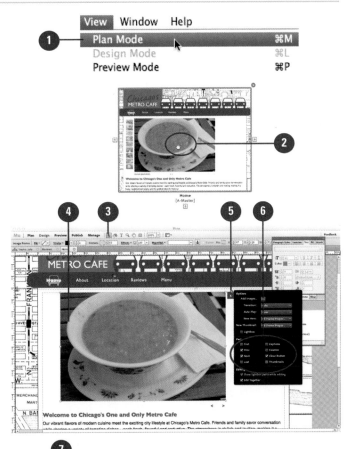

Embedding Arbitrary HTML

11

Introduction

Another great feature in Muse is the ability to embed arbitrary HTML, which you can acquire from popular sites such as Google Maps, YouTube, Flickr, and Twitter. All of these sites include widgets such as maps and videos that you can copy and paste into Muse.

In this chapter, you'll learn how to access arbitrary HTML from third-party sites and copy/paste the code into your Muse layouts. You'll learn how to embed a custom size Google Map, as well as how to insert videos from popular sites such as YouTube, Flickr, and Hulu.

This chapter also shows you how to set up a custom Twitter Search Widget and embed it in Muse. The final section explains how to access and edit the arbitrary HTML code after you've pasted it into your site.

Inserting a Google Map

Copy and paste arbitrary HTML

① Choose **Plan Mode** from the **View** menu.

TIMESAVER *Press Cmd+M (Mac) or Ctrl+M (Win) to apply the Plan Mode command quickly.*

② From the sitemap, double-click the thumbnail of the page you'd like to add a Google map to.

Muse opens the page in Design Mode.

③ Click the **Rectangle Tool** icon at the top of the Design Mode interface.

TIMESAVER *Press M to access the Rectangle tool quickly.*

④ Click and drag on the page with the **Rectangle** tool to create a rectangle about the size you would like the Google map to be.

⑤ Note the rectangle dimensions displayed in the **Width** and **Height** fields of the Control panel.

⑥ Choose **Edit > Clear** or press **Delete** or **Backspace** (Win).

Including a Google map in your site is a lot easier than you might think. Google Maps includes a customize feature, which enables you to assign a custom size to the map. After you determine a zoom percentage and size for the map, you can copy the HTML code to the Clipboard and then paste the map directly onto your site page. When you do, Muse automatically detects the source tags and pastes the code as HTML on the page.

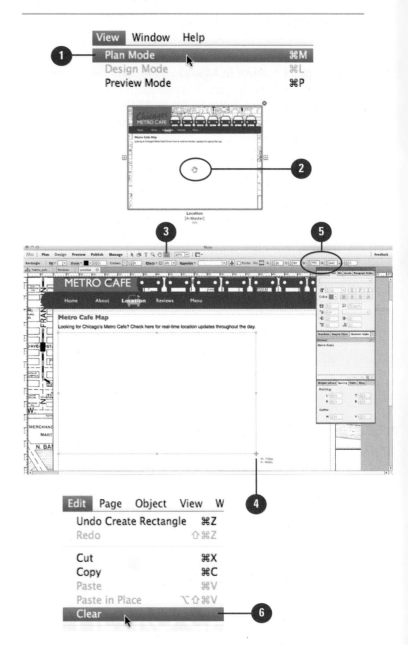

7. In your preferred browser, visit **maps.google.com**.

8. Enter the street address or zip code in the Search field at the top of the page.

9. Use the **Zoom In/Zoom Out** controls to apply the desired zoom percentage for the map.

10. Click the **link** button (the link icon) to display a flyout Link window.

11. Click the **Customize and Preview Embedded Map** link.

    Google Maps displays the Customize info in a separate browser window.

12. Under **Map Size**, choose **Custom**.

13. Enter the **Width** and **Height** settings that you noted earlier in step 5.

14. Place the cursor in the HTML field located at the bottom of the window and choose **Edit > Select All**.

    TIMESAVER *Press Cmd+A (Mac) or Ctrl+A (Win) to apply the Select All command quickly.*

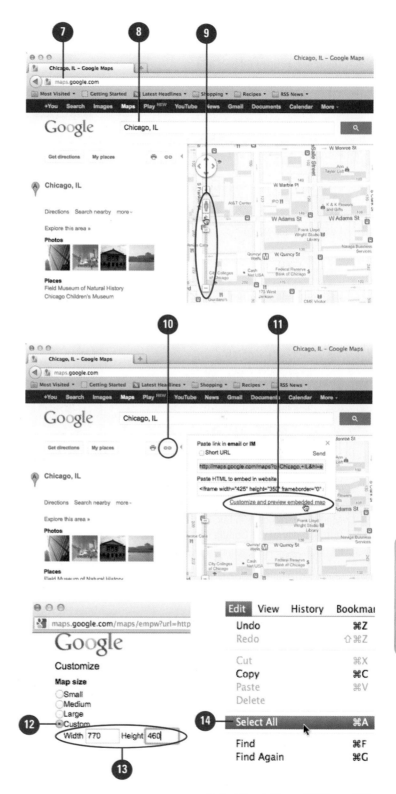

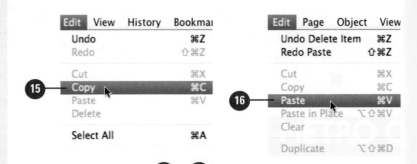

15 To copy the selected HTML to the Clipboard, choose **Edit > Copy**.

TIMESAVER *Press Cmd+C (Mac) or Ctrl+C (Win) to apply the Copy command quickly.*

16 Return to Muse and choose **Edit > Paste**.

TIMESAVER *Press Cmd+V (Mac) or Ctrl+V (Win) to apply the Paste command quickly.*

Muse pastes the Google map onto the page.

17 Click the **Selection Tool** icon at the top of the Design Mode interface.

TIMESAVER *Press V to access the Selection tool quickly.*

18 Click and drag with the **Selection** tool to position the map where you would like it on the page.

19 Choose **View > Preview Mode** or click the **Preview** button located in the upper left of the Design Mode interface.

Muse opens the page in Preview Mode, where you can test the functionality of the Google map.

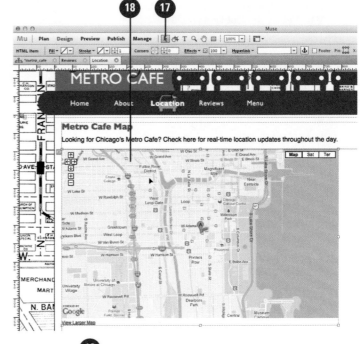

Inserting a YouTube, Flickr, or Hulu Video

Not only does Muse enable you to easily embed Google Maps at your sites, but you can also embed videos from popular sites such as YouTube, Flickr, and Hulu. Each of these sites contains an Embed feature that gives you access to arbitrary HTML. After you choose the video size, you can copy the HTML code to the Clipboard and then paste the video directly onto your site page.

Copy and paste arbitrary HTML

1. Choose **Plan Mode** from the **View** menu.

   TIMESAVER *Press Cmd+M (Mac) or Ctrl+M (Win) to apply the Plan Mode command quickly.*

2. From the sitemap, double-click the thumbnail of the page you'd like to add a video to.

   Muse opens the page in Design Mode.

3. In your preferred browser, visit YouTube, Flickr, or Hulu, and locate the video you would like to embed in Muse.

4. Click the **Share** button (YouTube and Flickr) or the **More** button (Hulu) to display the Embed button.

5. Click the **Embed** button to display the HTML code that you can copy and paste.

6. Choose the video size.

   IMPORTANT *YouTube and Flickr enable you to enter custom width and height settings, while Hulu does not. To do this at Flickr, click the Customize the Player button.*

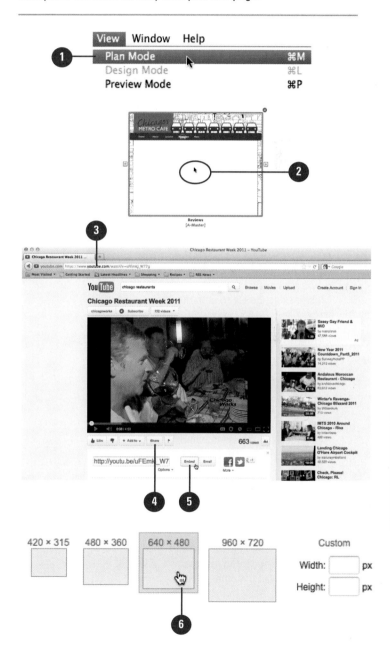

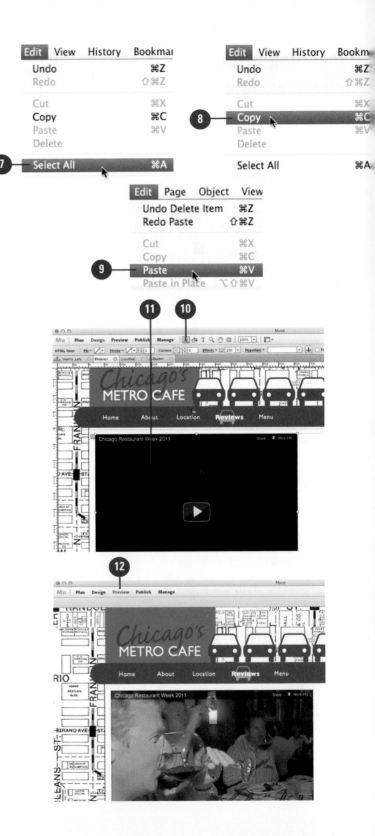

(7) Place the cursor in the HTML field and choose **Edit > Select All**.

TIMESAVER *Press Cmd+A (Mac) or Ctrl+A (Win) to apply the Select All command quickly.*

(8) To copy the selected HTML to the Clipboard, choose **Edit > Copy**.

TIMESAVER *Press Cmd+C (Mac) or Ctrl+C (Win) to apply the Copy command quickly.*

IMPORTANT *Hulu includes a Copy Embed Code button that you can use instead of the Edit > Copy command.*

(9) Return to Muse and choose **Edit > Paste**.

TIMESAVER *Press Cmd+V (Mac) or Ctrl+V (Win) to apply the Paste command quickly.*

Muse pastes the video onto the page.

(10) Click the **Selection Tool** icon at the top of the Design Mode interface.

TIMESAVER *Press V to access the Selection tool quickly.*

(11) Click and drag with the **Selection** tool to position the video where you would like it on the page.

(12) Choose **View > Preview Mode** or click the **Preview** button located in the upper left of the Design Mode interface.

Muse opens the page in Preview Mode, where you can test the functionality of the embedded video.

Inserting a Twitter Search Widget

You can also incorporate social media into your websites by inserting a Twitter Search Widget. This special widget displays posts from various Twitter users based on your predefined search criteria. To insert one of these widgets, you must first visit the widgets resource page at Twitter.com and choose the preferred Search Widget options, such as search query, title, and caption. You can even customize the widget's appearance to better suit your website's design. You can then copy the HTML code to the Clipboard and paste the Search Widget directly onto your site page.

Copy and paste arbitrary HTML

1 Choose **Plan Mode** from the **View** menu.

> **TIMESAVER** *Press Cmd+M (Mac) or Ctrl+M (Win) to apply the Plan Mode command quickly.*

2 From the sitemap, double-click the thumbnail of the page you'd like to add a Twitter Search Widget to.

Muse opens the page in Design Mode.

3 In your preferred browser, visit **http://twitter.com/about/resources/widgets**.

4 Click the **My Website** button.

5 Click the **Search Widget** link.

6 Enter a keyword in the **Search Query** field.

7 Enter a title in the **Title** field.

8 Enter a caption in the **Caption** field.

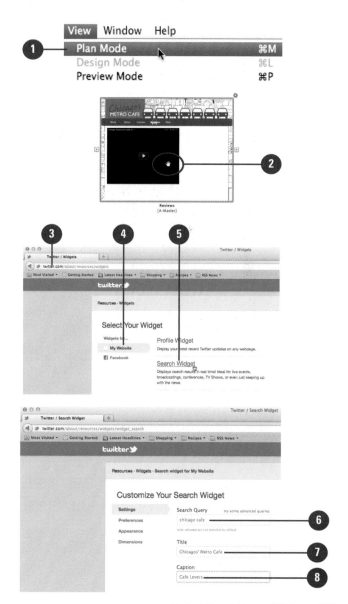

9. Click the **Appearance** button.

10. Choose the preferred background, text, and link colors.

11. Click the **Finish & Grab Code** button.

12. Place the cursor in the HTML field and choose **Edit > Select All**.

    TIMESAVER *Press Cmd+A (Mac) or Ctrl+A (Win) to apply the Select All command quickly.*

13. To copy the selected HTML to the Clipboard, choose **Edit > Copy**.

    TIMESAVER *Press Cmd+C (Mac) or Ctrl+C (Win) to apply the Copy command quickly.*

14. Return to Muse and choose **Edit > Paste**.

    TIMESAVER *Press Cmd+V (Mac) or Ctrl+V (Win) to apply the Paste command quickly.*

    Muse pastes the Twitter Search Widget onto the page.

15 Click the **Selection Tool** icon at the top of the Design Mode interface.

TIMESAVER *Press V to access the Selection tool quickly.*

16 Click and drag with the **Selection** tool to position the Twitter Search Widget where you would like it on the page.

17 Choose **View > Preview Mode** or click the **Preview** button located in the upper left of the Design Mode interface.

Muse opens the page in Preview Mode, where you can test the functionality of the embedded Twitter Search Widget.

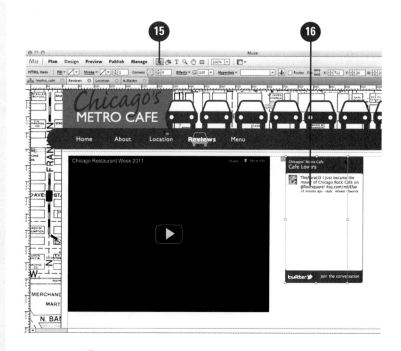

Editing Arbitrary Code in Muse

You can edit the size of an embedded map, video, or other widget even after you've pasted the arbitrary HTML into your site. To do so, right-click or Control-click (Mac) the widget on the page and choose HTML from the contextual menu. This displays the HTML Code dialog box. If you know basic HTML code, you can easily change the width and height values displayed in the top line of the code for the embedded widget.

Choose the HTML command from the contextual menu

① Choose **Plan Mode** from the **View** menu.

TIMESAVER *Press Cmd+M (Mac) or Ctrl+M (Win) to apply the Plan Mode command quickly.*

② From the sitemap, double-click the thumbnail of the page whose arbitrary HTML you'd like to edit.

Muse opens the page in Design Mode.

③ To access the contextual menu, right-click or Control-click (Mac) the embedded HTML object and choose **HTML**.

Muse displays the HTML Code dialog box.

④ Edit the code inside the HTML Code dialog box. For example, in the first line of code, you can resize the Google map by entering new values in the quotes next to where it reads width = and height =.

⑤ Click **OK** to close the HTML Code dialog box.

Muse updates the embedded HTML.

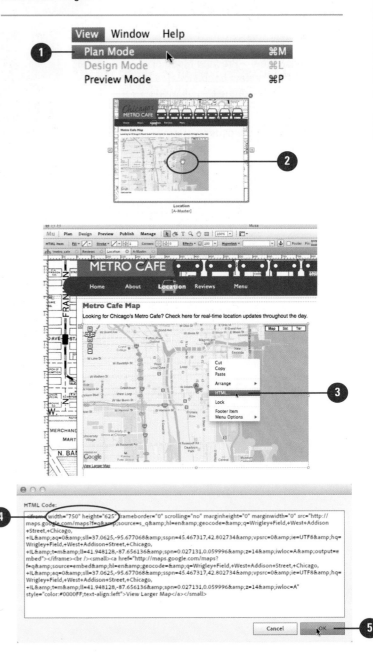

Previewing a Site

12

Introduction

As you design web pages in Muse, it's essential to test the functionality of each page element you've included in your design, such as navigational buttons, hyperlinks, and slideshows. Muse comes equipped with a Preview Mode, which enables you to test your sites from within the application. However, to ensure proper functionality, you should also preview your sites in some external browsers, such as Google Chrome, Apple Safari, Mozilla Firefox, and Windows Internet Explorer.

The Preview Mode in Muse uses WebKit as its rendering engine. This is the same engine that powers Apple Safari, Google Chrome, and most mobile phone browsers.

In this chapter, you will learn how to preview individual pages and entire websites using Preview Mode. You'll also learn how to preview them using your system's default web browser application.

The final section of this chapter explains how to use the Export as HTML command to preview your websites in a non-default browser application.

Previewing a Page in Muse

Although it's always a good idea to preview web pages in a browser, Muse also includes a Preview Mode, which enables you to render pages right inside the Muse application. Preview uses WebKit as its rendering engine. This is the same engine that powers Apple Safari, Google Chrome, and most mobile phone browsers. You can open the current page in Preview by choosing Preview Mode from the View menu, or by clicking the Preview button in the upper-left corner of the interface.

Choose the Preview command

① Choose **Plan Mode** from the **View** menu.

   TIMESAVER *Press Cmd+M (Mac) or Ctrl+M (Win) to apply the Plan Mode command quickly.*

② From the sitemap, double-click the thumbnail of the page you'd like to preview.

   Muse opens the page in Design Mode.

③ Choose **View > Preview Mode** or click the **Preview** button located in the upper left of the Design Mode interface.

   TIMESAVER *Press Cmd+P (Mac) or Ctrl+P (Win) to apply the Preview Mode command quickly.*

   Muse displays the current page in Preview Mode.

Did You Know?

You can also enter Preview Mode by clicking the Preview button. To display the current page in Preview Mode, click the Preview button located in the upper left of the Design Mode interface.

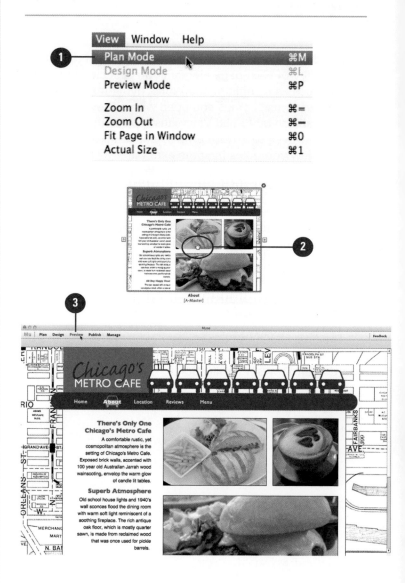

Previewing a Site in Muse

Not only can you render a single web page in Preview Mode—you can also preview the entire site! If you click a page's navigational buttons while in Preview Mode, Muse takes you to the pages, just as if you were previewing the site in a browser. Note that depending on the amount of content placed on each page, the site rendering may be a bit slower in Preview Mode than when previewing the site in an actual browser.

Choose the Preview command

1. Choose **Plan Mode** from the **View** menu.

   TIMESAVER *Press Cmd+M (Mac) or Ctrl+M (Win) to apply the Plan Mode command quickly.*

2. From the sitemap, double-click the thumbnail of any page in the site.

   Muse opens the page in Design Mode.

3. Choose **View > Preview Mode** or click the **Preview** button located in the upper left of the Design Mode interface.

   TIMESAVER *Press Cmd+P (Mac) or Ctrl+P (Win) to apply the Preview Mode command quickly.*

   Muse displays the current page in Preview Mode.

4. To display each page of the site in Preview Mode, click the navigational buttons.

Did You Know?

You can also enter Preview Mode by clicking the Preview button. To display the current page in Preview Mode, click the Preview button located in the upper left of the Design Mode interface.

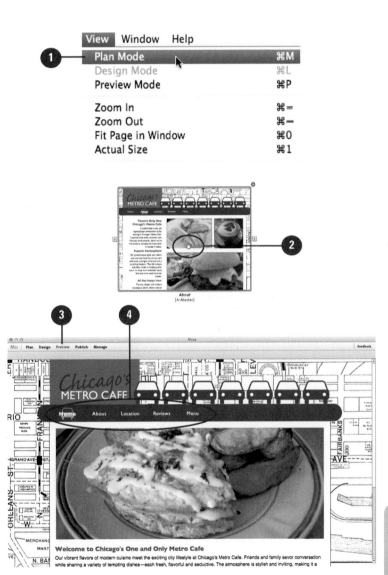

Previewing a Page in the Default Browser

Although the Preview Mode in Muse is incredibly accurate, it is not able to emulate the behavior of every browser, especially Mozilla Firefox and Windows Internet Explorer; therefore, you should still always preview your pages in every browser available. Doing so helps you ensure that all the page elements will function properly when publishing the site to the Web. To preview the current page in your system's default browser application, choose Preview Page in Browser from the File menu.

Choose the Preview Page in Browser command

1 Choose **Plan Mode** from the **View** menu.

> **TIMESAVER** Press Cmd+M (Mac) or Ctrl+M (Win) to apply the Plan Mode command quickly.

2 From the sitemap, double-click the thumbnail of the page you'd like to preview in a browser.

Muse opens the page in Design Mode.

3 Choose **File > Preview Page in Browser.**

> **TIMESAVER** Press Shift+Cmd+E (Mac) or Shift+Ctrl+E (Win) to apply the Preview Page in Browser command quickly.

Muse creates a temporary export and displays the current page in your system's default browser.

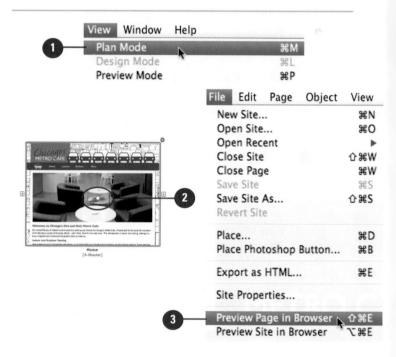

Muse displays the current page in your system's default browser.

Previewing a Site in the Default Browser

Before you publish your site to the Web, it's always a good idea to preview it in a browser. Doing so enables you to make sure that all of your navigational buttons, hyperlinks, and slideshows are functioning properly. When you choose the Preview Site in Browser command, Muse creates a temporary site export, which enables you to view the site in your system's default browser application.

Choose the Preview Site in Browser command

1. Choose **Plan Mode** from the **View** menu.

   TIMESAVER *Press Cmd+M (Mac) or Ctrl+M (Win) to apply the Plan Mode command quickly.*

2. Choose **File > Preview Site in Browser.**

   TIMESAVER *Press Option+Cmd+E (Mac) or Option+Ctrl+E (Win) to apply the Preview Site in Browser command quickly.*

   Muse creates a temporary export and displays the current page in your system's default browser.

3. To display each page of the site in the default browser, click the navigational buttons.

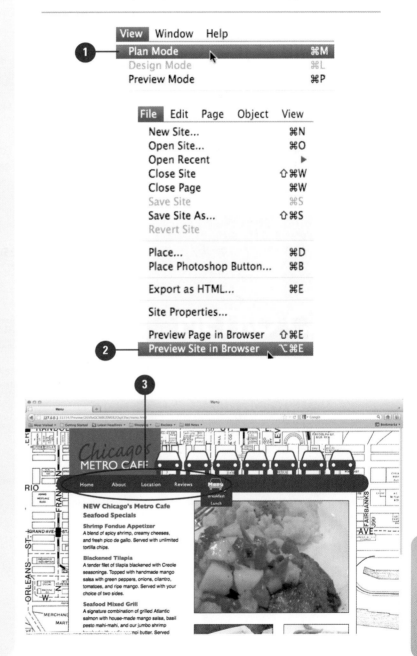

Previewing in a Non-Default Browser

To test a website accurately before publishing it, you should preview it in as many browsers as possible—not just in your system's default browser. In order to do this in Muse, you must choose the Export as HTML command. After you export the site as HTML, you can open the index.html page (the first page of the site) in all of the other browsers on your system, such as Google Chrome, Apple Safari, Mozilla Firefox, and Windows Internet Explorer.

Choose the Export as HTML command

① Choose **Plan Mode** from the **View** menu.

> **TIMESAVER** *Press Cmd+M (Mac) or Ctrl+M (Win) to apply the Plan Mode command quickly.*

② Choose **File > Export as HTML**.

> **TIMESAVER** *Press Cmd+E (Mac) or Ctrl+E (Win) to apply the Export as HTML command quickly.*

Muse displays the Export to HTML dialog box.

> **IMPORTANT** *If any of the placed graphics in the site have been moved or deleted from where they were originally stored on your computer, they appear as missing or modified. In this instance, when you choose the Export as HTML command, Muse displays a warning dialog box, reminding you to link them in the Assets panel before exporting.*

③ In the Export to HTML dialog box that appears, Muse tells you where the export folder will be saved on your system disk. Click **OK** to export the site.

Muse exports the site to the location displayed in the Export to HTML dialog box.

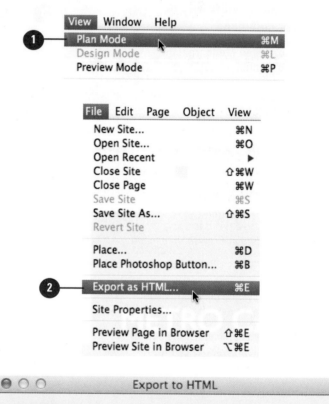

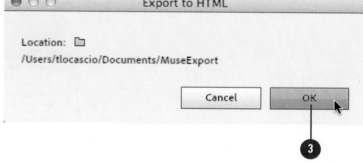

④ Click **OK** to close the Export to HTML dialog box.

IMPORTANT *Do not click the View Site button. Doing so will open the site in the default browser.*

⑤ Launch the non-default web browser application you would like to preview the site in, such as Google Chrome, Apple Safari, Mozilla Firefox, or Windows Internet Explorer, and choose **Open File** from the browser **File** menu.

⑥ In the Open file dialog box that appears, navigate to the **Muse Export** folder location and select the **index.html** file.

⑦ Click **Open** to display the first page of the site in the non-default browser.

⑧ To display each page of the site in the non-default browser, click the navigational buttons.

Publishing a Site with Muse

Introduction

The final step when creating a website in Muse is to make it visible online. Thankfully, through its association with Adobe's Business Catalyst service, you can upload a trial version of a website directly from Muse to a temporary URL at businesscatalyst.com.

When you first install Muse, a free Business Catalyst account is automatically created for you. As a result, any time you choose the Publish command or click the Publish button, you are automatically signed in to the Business Catalyst service.

This chapter explains how to use the Publish feature in Muse to post a free, 30-day trial version of your site at businesscatalyst.com. One of the great things about this free service is that you can email the temporary URL to your clients. Trial sites are great for making client presentations, gathering critiques, and requesting site approval.

You'll also learn how to make site edits and update what's been posted online at the temporary Business Catalyst URL. The final section of this chapter explains how to perform a final HTML export, which you can then upload to a hosting service other than Business Catalyst.

What You'll Do

Publishing a Trial Site

Updating Changes to a Published Trial Site

Exporting HTML

Publishing a Trial Site

Choose the Publish command

1. Choose **Plan Mode** from the **View** menu.

   TIMESAVER *Press Cmd+M (Mac) or Ctrl+M (Win) to apply the Plan Mode command quickly.*

2. From the **File** menu, choose **Publish**.

   TIMESAVER *Press Option+Cmd+P (Mac) or Alt+Ctrl+P (Win) to apply the Publish command quickly. You can also click the Publish button in the upper left of the Muse interface.*

   IMPORTANT *If the website contains missing or modified graphics, Muse displays a warning dialog box reminding you that they should be updated before publishing. You can update missing or modified graphics via the Assets panel (see Chapter 5, "Working with Graphics").*

   Muse displays the Publish dialog box.

3. Enter a name for the website project in the **Site Name** field. This is what Business Catalyst uses for the trial site URL.

   IMPORTANT *Muse displays the actual URL that will be assigned to the site directly underneath the Site Name field.*

4. To display additional publishing options, click the **Options** button.

When you install Muse and enter an email and password, a free Adobe Business Catalyst account is automatically set up for you. You can use this service to upload a trial version of the website you've created in Muse. The trial version is posted for free at the Business Catalyst site for 30 days. You can send the assigned trial URL to your clients for approval of your site design. When you're ready to post the site officially, you can either upgrade the site at Business Catalyst and pay an additional hosting fee, or you can use a different hosting service.

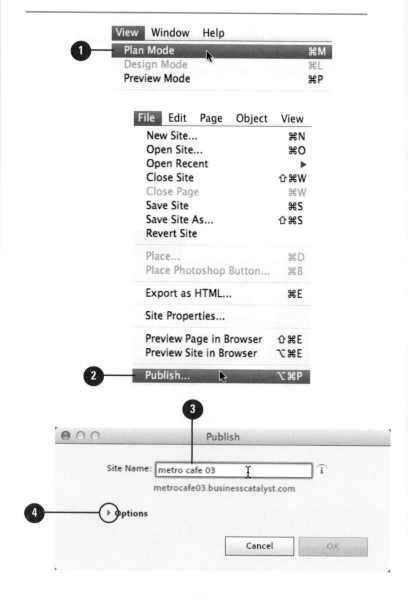

5 Choose **New Site** from the **Publish To** drop-down list.

IMPORTANT *Muse automatically enters the site name in the URL field*

6 Click **OK** to upload the trial site to your Business Catalyst account.

As soon as the upload is complete, Muse displays the online trial site in your default browser.

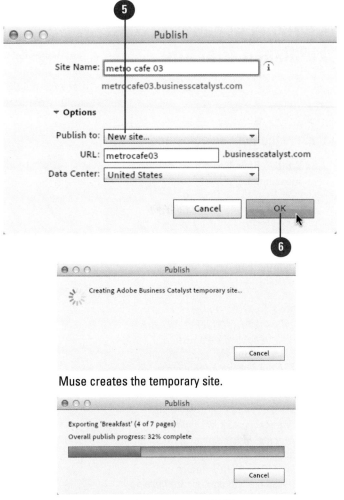

Muse creates the temporary site.

Muse uploads the temporary site files.

Muse displays the online trial site in your default browser.

Updating Changes to a Published Trial Site

After you post a trial version of a website at businesscatalyst.com, your clients may ask you to make additional edits to the site's content and/or functionality. To do so, you can make the edits in Design Mode and then publish just the modified files to the Business Catalyst trial URL. Your clients can then view the changes by revisiting the trial site in a browser.

Choose the Publish command

1. Choose **Plan Mode** from the **View** menu.

   TIMESAVER Press Cmd+M (Mac) or Ctrl+M (Win) to apply the Plan Mode command quickly.

2. From the **File** menu, choose **Publish**.

   TIMESAVER Press Option+Cmd+P (Mac) or Alt+Ctrl+P (Win) to apply the Publish command quickly. You can also click the Publish button in the upper left of the Muse interface.

   IMPORTANT *If the website contains missing or modified graphics, Muse displays a warning dialog box reminding you that they should be updated before publishing. You can update missing or modified graphics via the Assets panel (see Chapter 5, "Working with Graphics").*

   Muse displays the Publish dialog box.

3. To display additional publishing options, click the **Options** button.

4. Choose the site name from the **Publish To** drop-down list.

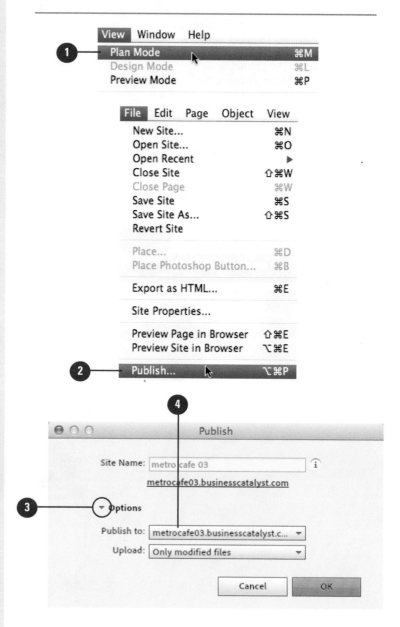

5 Choose **Only Modified Files** from the **Upload** drop-down list.

6 Click **OK** to update the trial site at your Business Catalyst account.

As soon as the upload is complete, Muse displays the online trial site in your default browser.

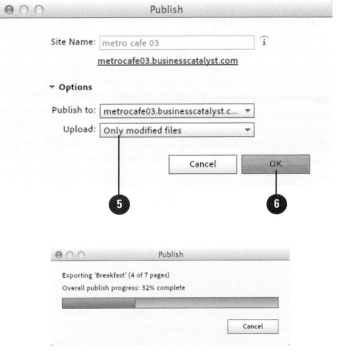

Muse uploads the temporary site files.

Muse displays the updated trial site in your default browser.

Exporting HTML

When the website is finally complete and you are ready to post it online using a service other than Business Catalyst, you must perform a final HTML export. When you do, Muse generates all the HTML, CSS, and optimized graphics and places them in a folder. After you purchase a URL for the site, you must upload all the contents of this final export folder to your hosting server.

Choose the Export as HTML command

① Choose **Plan Mode** from the **View** menu.

> **TIMESAVER** *Press Cmd+M (Mac) or Ctrl+M (Win) to apply the Plan Mode command quickly.*

② Choose **File > Export as HTML.**

> **TIMESAVER** *Press Cmd+E (Mac) or Ctrl+E (Win) to apply the Export as HTML command quickly.*

Muse displays the Export to HTML dialog box.

> **IMPORTANT** *If any of the placed graphics in the site are not linked when you choose the Export as HTML command, Muse displays a warning dialog box, reminding you to link them in the Assets panel before exporting.*

③ To choose a system location for the export folder, click the **Location** folder icon.

Muse displays the Select Local Folder to Export dialog box.

④ Navigate to the preferred location on your system disk.

⑤ Click the **New Folder** button.

Muse displays the New Folder dialog box.

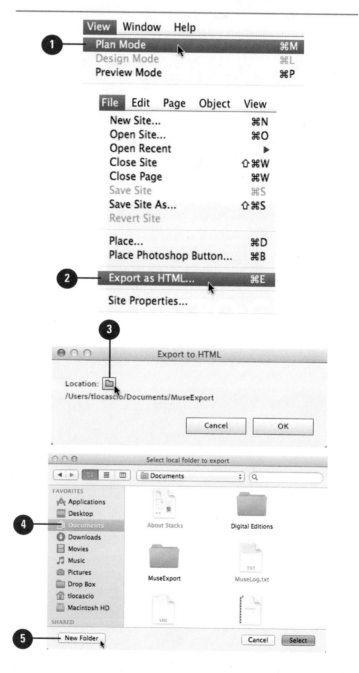

6 Enter a name for the export folder.

7 Click **Create**.

8 Click **Select**.

9 Click **OK** to export the site.

Muse exports the site to the location displayed in the Export to HTML dialog box.

10 When the site is finished exporting, click **OK** again to close the Export to HTML dialog box.

IMPORTANT *Muse is unlike Adobe Dreamweaver, in that you cannot use it to upload a site to any other hosting service other than Business Catalyst. If you are using another hosting service, you can upload the exported site using FTP client software. FileZilla is an excellent FTP client that is not only free, but is also available for both platforms (Mac and Windows).*

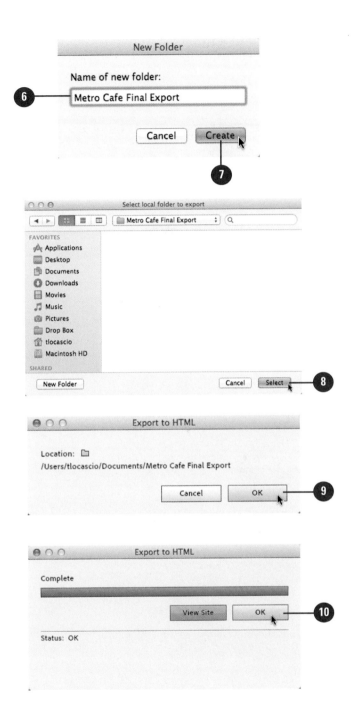

Index

Symbols

+ (plus symbol)
   in graphic styles, 99
   style overrides, 126, 128
100% browser width, displaying
   graphics at, 86

A

accounts, Creative Cloud, creating, 5-8
Active rollover state images, inserting,
   62-63
Actual Size command, 23
Add Images button, 152-153
Add New Master Page command, 36
Add New Top Level Page command, 33
Adobe Application Manager, 5-8
Adobe Muse
   downloading installer, 5-8
   installing, 5-8
   launching, 9-10
   subscriptions, purchasing, 2-4
alignment (text), 111
anchor links
   applying, 145-146
   creating, 144
applying
   anchor links, 145-146
   bold text, 110

character styles, 124-125
font styles, 110
graphic styles, 100-101
italic text, 110
link styles, 142-143
master pages, 45-46
paragraph styles, 126-127
span tags, 133-134
underlined text, 110
arbitrary HTML
   editing, 176
   Google Maps, inserting, 168-170
   Twitter Search Widgets, inserting,
     173-175
   YouTube/Flickr/Hulu videos,
     inserting, 171-172
Auto Play options in slideshows/
   compositions, 162

B

background color, filling browser
   with, 42
background image, filling browser
   with, 43-44
Bar Menu widget, 53
bevel effects, 93-94
bold text, applying, 110
browser location, pinning graphics
   to, 85